D0397199

COPING WITH

Teenage
Motherhood

COPING WITH

Teenage

Motherhood

Carolyn Simpson

THE ROSEN PUBLISHING GROUP, INC./NEW YORK

Published in 1992 by The Rosen Publishing Group, Inc.
29 East 21st Street, New York, NY 10010

Copyright 1992 by Carolyn Simpson

First Edition

Library of Congress Cataloging-in-Publication Data

Simpson, Carolyn.
    Coping with teenage motherhood / Carolyn Simpson.
      p. cm.
    Includes bibliographical references and index.
    Summary: Provides information and advice on how to cope as a teenage
mother before and after the baby is born.
    ISBN 0-8239-1458-5
    1. Teenage mothers—United States—Life skills guides—Juvenile
literature. [1. Teenage mothers. 2. Pregnancy.]   I. Title.
HQ759.4.S568   1992
306.85′6—dc20   92-8168
                                                            CIP
                                                             AC

Manufactured in the United States of America

ABOUT THE AUTHOR ◇

Carolyn Simpson is an adjunct instructor of Psychology at Tulsa Junior College, Tulsa, Oklahoma. She has worked in the mental health field since 1973, principally as a clinical social worker. She also taught and counseled in an alternative high school program originally designed for pregnant and parenting teens in Bridgton, Maine.

She received a bachelor's degree from Colby College, Waterville, Maine, and a master's in Human Relations from the University of Oklahoma. She has written several other books in this series: *Coping with an Unplanned Pregnancy*, *Coping with Emotional Disorders*, and *Careers in Social Work*, the last two with her husband.

She lives with her husband, their three children, and their dogs, Lion and Wolf, on the outskirts of Tulsa.

Acknowledgments

Many people have helped me prepare this book. I am profoundly grateful to the Planned Parenthood organization of Tulsa for its information and willingness to answer my questions, to MEND—the Crisis Pregnancy Center of Broken Arrow, Oklahoma, for its help, and especially to the teens at the Margaret Hudson School of Tulsa, who shared so much advice. Thanks to Jan Figart, the executive director of this innovative and tremendously successful school, for her time and helpfulness.

And to my friends: Becky, Shelly, Lisa, and Lisa, who shared their thoughts and experiences with me, my special thanks.

Contents

Preface

If you have just discovered you're pregnant, you may be wondering what's the point of reading about the subject. After all, you can't undo the pregnancy. What's done is done.

This book has two purposes. The first is to *educate* you about the unfolding process of pregnancy, birth, and the raising of a child.

But more than that, it is intended to show you that there are many ways to face the experience, and that when something bad happens (maybe your parents throw you out or your boyfriend dumps you), there are still alternatives. If your family can't support you (emotionally or financially), there are agencies that can help. If you can't afford prenatal care, *again*, there are resources open to you. If you discover that your infant isn't the sweet little doll you expected, there are people and books to help you learn to cope.

I don't pretend to know the answers to every situation, but I have a wealth of experience (having had four children myself); and when I didn't know something, the many pregnant and parenting teens from the Margaret Hudson School provided me with their experience and advice.

So read this book to familiarize yourself with all the facets of pregnancy, birth, and early childrearing. Use the books listed in For Further Reading to read up on certain subjects in greater depth. At the end of each chapter I've included "Advice from Teen Moms," comments that parenting teens gave me to pass on to you. More than anything else, these girls wanted me to tell you, "Don't give up! It WILL get better."

CHAPTER 1

You're Pregnant:

Now What?

For the sake of this chapter, let's assume you didn't plan this pregnancy. Or at least, you, your boyfriend, and your parents didn't plan it together. You've been sexually active and not very careful. Assuming that you're well attuned to your menstrual cycle, when you discover that your period is over two weeks late you're going to start feeling suspicious. And nervous . . .

Before you verify what you suspect, these are the symptoms you might encounter. Usually, the first tipoff to pregnancy is lateness of your period or a slight amount of bleeding about the time your period was due. Some girls complain that their breasts "tingle"; it's a feeling akin to that when your period is about to start, but it doesn't start. Your breasts simply go on feeling tingly and sensitive.

Perhaps you haven't noticed that your period is overdue, and perhaps you don't experience any breast sensations. But it's hard to ignore nausea and vomiting—common symptoms of early pregnancy. Some people wake up feeling queasy; some stay queasy all day; some feel queasy only at mealtimes. Unfortunately, some teens convince themselves that they feel sick because they're nervous, under a lot of stress, or catching the flu. If the nausea is accompanied by a need to go to the bathroom more frequently, they may tell themselves they have a bladder infection, which itself is reason enough to see a doctor.

I can't stress this enough: If you even suspect you're pregnant (and *any unprotected act of intercourse* can lead to pregnancy), find out for sure immediately. Pretending that the symptoms mean something else won't make the pregnancy go away. Simply not wanting to be pregnant won't make it go away either. Finding out early—verifying the pregnancy—gives you options and the opportunity to seek early prenatal care, which will result in a better pregnancy and a healthier baby.

Pregnancy Tests

So how do you find out for sure whether or not you're pregnant? You can check it out in a variety of ways. It depends on whether you want to remain anonymous, spend some money, or spend none at all. To check it out in secrecy, you can buy one of the home pregnancy tests available in drugstores or supermarkets. They cost from $11 to $17, depending on the brand and whether the kit contains one or two tests. The good points of these kits are that you can use them in privacy, they're more accurate these days, and they can be used as early as two or three days after your period was due. They're also easier to read these days. The bad point is that if you do the test in privacy you have no support person to help you *deal* with the news. If you want someone available to give you advice, your best bet is to go to a clinic that offers pregnancy testing and follow-up care. You can find these clinics in the Yellow Pages of your phone book under Birth Control or Pregnancy Counseling or Family Planning. The services are almost always free, and you can get the verdict (positive or negative) in a matter of minutes. If positive, you can talk to a professional about your options.

If you don't mind going to your family physician and you can afford it, that is an option. The nurse will probably run the test on your urine (more than likely using a test similar to the kits you can buy). The doctor may then give you a physical exam.

Each method (seeing your doctor, going to a clinic, or using a test kit at home) has its advantages and disadvantages. What matters is that you decide to *use one of them*. The longer you wait to detect your pregnancy, the fewer options you have.

Once you find out that you're pregnant, it may take some time to digest the news. Sure, everyone knows that having sex (even one time) can lead to pregnancy, but rarely do teenagers think it can happen to them. The sooner you accept the fact that you are indeed pregnant, the sooner you can start preparing for the event. Tests *can* be wrong, but if you've taken more than one and they have come back positive—and more important, if you have reason to be pregnant—then accept the fact and move on.

Coping with Feelings

Accepting the fact means dealing with an assortment of emotions. Perhaps you'll be shocked that "it could happen to me!"; perhaps you'll be angry at yourself—or at the guy—for not being more careful. Perhaps you'll wonder what's going to happen to your life now. You may be angry, confused, and depressed. "What am I going to do now?" You may be scared. "What are my folks going to say?" "How can I tell them?" Then again, you may be excited and pleased in some ways. A baby signifies to some people that you're an adult, hence, important. It proves that someone must have found you desirable, and that might bring a smile to your face. The reality of actually having created a life probably won't sink in right away.

First of all, accept all of your feelings. It's okay to be angry, distressed, and depressed. It's okay even to wish you weren't pregnant. Feelings alone won't hurt the baby. Feel the feelings, talk to a counselor who can help you deal with them, and then forgive yourself. Perhaps you made a mistake, but then, we all do from time to time. This will probably not be the only mistake in your life. Forgive your boyfriend too. Carrying around anger for the next nine months will be a waste of your time.

Next, consider your circumstances and set some goals. Do you want to marry the father of the baby? Does he want to marry you? Is that practical, or are you both too young and immature to handle the responsibilities that come with marriage? Is your partner someone you want to wake up with for the next fifty years or so, because that's how long a teenage marriage can last. If you can't envision living with this guy or you suspect he won't remain faithful to you (or you won't remain faithful to him) for the long haul, then consider other possibilities. Getting pregnant may have been a mistake, but don't make it worse by marrying someone you don't really like. Young people do much of their growing and changing in their early twenties, so you two may become very different people in the next five to ten years.

Sometimes it takes a wise person to consider options other than marriage. Abortion (which to date is still legal) comes with its own set of problems. Adoption may allow you some say as to where your baby ends up, or it may not. Many of you will choose single parenting—with or without your parents' help.

Breaking the News

First, tell your boyfriend. After all, it's his baby too. If the father is only an acquaintance, not someone with whom you want to spend your life negotiating child support, you might choose to tell your parents first. In the heat of anger and regret we sometimes fail to do things we later wish we had done, and vice versa. You may want or need his financial support somewhere down the line.

Telling your parents is a tricky matter for most people. I know one girl who didn't tell her folks until she was almost eight months pregnant because she feared their reaction. I kept wondering what was going to happen when the baby came? Was she going to murmur, "Oh, by the way, I'm having a baby now"? The longer you put off telling them, the harder it will be. Get it over with. Pick a time when neither you nor they will be distracted. In other words, don't blurt out the news as they're hustling off to work in the morning. You might wait until the evening dishes are done and your parents are relaxing, maybe with the newspaper or a book. Don't interrupt if they're watching a favorite television program; they'll be annoyed with you before you even begin. Mention that you have something important to discuss with them, and have your first few words memorized. There's nothing more annoying (and I speak now as a parent) than having your child demand your attention and then lose her ability to speak so that you have to drag the bad news out of her. Tell them that you're pregnant and how you're feeling about it. Expect them to go a little crazy. Parents want their children to have a better life than theirs. Discovering that you're pregnant may be more than they can take in right away. Let them express their feelings as long as they aren't abusive to you, and if you want their help, consider your options together. Will you remain with them and raise the baby at home? Will they take over the childrearing? After the initial shock has worn off, chances are your parents will handle the news better than you think.

On the other hand, if you come from a dysfunctional family and your parents are not particularly interested in your welfare or a baby's, talk to a counselor first to decide how best to approach them. The people at family planning clinics are usually willing to help a teenager tell her parents. No matter how much you fear their anger or resentment, take this step and continue to set goals.

Prenatal Care

The urgency about confirming your pregnancy and telling the appropriate people lies in the importance of getting prenatal care as early as possible. Tests need to be done to identify any health problems you may have and to pinpoint any risks attached to the pregnancy. Failure to obtain prompt prenatal care can lead to birth complications, a premature baby, or a low-weight baby. If money is a problem (as it is for a majority of teenagers in your position), consider the family planning clinic, the city health department, or Planned Parenthood (a nationwide network of family planning clinics designed to help low-income people). These agencies can help you file for Title XIX benefits so that the government will pay your doctor and hospital bills. At Planned Parenthood, their doctors will treat you at a reduced charge depending on your financial need.

The clinic or doctor will make tests to determine whether you're disease-free (you certainly want to know if you've been exposed to a sexually transmitted disease) and healthy. Blood tests will show your blood type, your blood sugar level, your Rh factor, and whether or not you're immune to rubella—a dangerous virus to catch when you're pregnant. Later, an ultrasound test may be done to determine how the fetus is progressing and to further establish the date of delivery. I'll describe these tests in detail in later chapters. They are not scary (although having blood drawn may be unpleasant if you don't like needles), and they're important. The health of your baby depends on your being as healthy as possible yourself.

Continuing School

Along with considering your relationship with your parents, consider what will happen to your schooling. When I was a teenager it was understood that if a girl got pregnant she dropped out of school. No ifs, ands, or buts. That was the way it was. Nowadays it is realized that the worst thing a teenager can do is abandon her education.

Education is often what allows people to rise out of poverty. To give up your schooling and stay home waiting for the baby is a grave mistake.

Wonderful programs are available (which we'll explore in the next chapter) that can enable you to continue school and to learn valuable information about your pregnancy and about parenting skills. At the very least, most school districts can provide you with a tutor.

School may seem like one more burden that you don't want to deal with—all those kids staring at you and whispering, all that "expanding" you're going to do right before their eyes. And how will you be able to concentrate anyway when your life is changing so drastically? But don't make a snap decision. It's much harder to return and pick up where you left off than it is to hang in there in the first place.

There are alternatives to almost every problem you can think up. There are separate schools for pregnant and parenting teens, so that you don't have to face non-pregnant teenagers while you study. There are separate schools to learn about proper nutrition and stress reduction while you're pregnant, and places where you can bond with other teenagers who are in similar circumstances. Most of all, by continuing your education in these special programs, you will end up a better parent as well as student.

Think about it. If you drop out of school to become a mother, how will you support yourself and your child should your parents stop supporting you or your boyfriend not come through? Do you think a minimum-wage job will support a family for long? Do you think you can always get welfare and food stamps? Do you have any idea how little that covers? Better to beef up your support system and learn a trade or prepare for a career. In this day and age, it is best to rely on yourself. Sometimes, that's all we can count on.

Advice from Teen Moms

1. "Be open with the father about the pregnancy. Don't keep it a secret from people close to you."
2. "Don't expect it to be easy; it won't be."
3. "Just because you're pregnant doesn't mean you have to marry. If you're not sure you want kids, there is always adoption. It is much better to place a child in love and security than to keep it in unstable conditions."
4. "Don't look down on yourself."
5. "Get medical care as soon as you become pregnant."
6. "Continue with your life. Finish school."

CHAPTER ◇ 2

Who's Going To
Help You?

Facing teenage parenthood is scary. After all, you've barely finished being a child yourself, and soon you'll be expected to take on all the responsibilities of an adult. There is a "downside" to being an adult, you know. But here we are going to see ways of beefing up your support system so that you don't have to face what's coming alone. The more committed people you have on your side during these next few months—and years—the better.

Naturally, you'll first want to consider how supportive the father of your baby is going to be. Is he someone you want to help you emotionally through the pregnancy? Would you want him with you at delivery? Not all guys can be counted on to come through in the labor and delivery room, whether you're married to them or not. Can this guy (or his family) help you financially? Regardless of whether it was a one-night stand, the man is obligated to support his child until it reaches maturity (legally defined as age eighteen). You may not want your boyfriend's emotional support, but don't immediately refuse his financial support. Remember, the pregnancy is probably going to be a shock to him, so give him time to adjust.

Let him be upset (as long as he isn't hurting you), and then wait for him to calm down. Whether or not you and he continue a relationship, he will always have an obligation to this child. That's a fact of life. If he's a guy who can also respond to your changing needs and you can lean on him, you are indeed fortunate. He'll have to grow up during this pregnancy, just as you'll be doing. There's nothing like growing up together. If he isn't supportive, however, you can't force it. You can expect financial support, but you can't make him love you or the child or what has happened to his life.

People on Your Side

Next consider for a moment who else is on your side. What about your parents? Assuming they are emotionally stable, think of them as your primary allies. Even if they are strapped for money, they can assist you in decision-making and help you find the right agencies to lend you financial support. Many girls have told me that their parents threw a fit when they first heard about the unplanned pregnancy but nonetheless came around, especially as it became obvious how much their help was needed. Some girls who were kicked out for having "gotten in trouble" were welcomed back into the household once the baby was born.

Your parents can help you in lots of ways. For one thing, it's a relief just to be able to share your unexpected news. Using your energy to plan for the baby is certainly better than using it to guard a "secret." Even if you think your parents are the most ignorant people on earth, they have more experience than you by virtue of having been around a lot longer. If you're willing to listen to them, they may help prepare you for your upcoming role: what you'll need to buy for a new baby, the medical care he or she will need, how to save your sanity when the baby doesn't sleep through the night.

If your parents are financially secure, they might help with the basic necessities for the baby that cost an arm and a leg. Even when parents seem to have trouble making ends meet, it's surprising how they can manage to feed and clothe one more person.

Parents can give you moral support while you're dealing with the pregnancy, they can give you financial support, and they can give you a sense of being nurtured yourself—that is, if they're able emotionally and financially to do so. Many parents are not.

What do you do if your parents are not willing or able to help you? Consider your relationship with the father of the baby. Is he someone with whom you'll maintain a relationship in the future, even if you don't marry? If so, how supportive can *his* parents be. Perhaps they'll want to be involved with their grandchild and are in a better position than your parents to lend financial support. Should your parents kick you out (as has happened to some girls), consider living with your boyfriend's parents.

Help from Friends

Dealing with friends is another tricky matter. You won't necessarily want to give up your old friends when you become pregnant, but you may find that your common ground fades fast. Whereas you're going to be preoccupied with your symptoms, worried about labor, and thinking about the new baby, they're going to lose interest after a while. No offense, but you're either going to start boring them or make them envious of your new role. Neither makes for a great friendship. Besides, your friends may start boring *you*, preoccupied as they are with school, dating, and parties. Because of your growing differences, you may wish for friends who share more similar circumstances. Pregnant women, whether in their teens or thirties, like to talk about what's going on with them and what lies ahead. And there's no one better to discuss it with than someone who is in the same boat or has recently been there.

You might consider cultivating new friends, found either in YWCA support groups or school parenting programs, to share these new experiences. But hang onto your old friends too. They may not have similar experiences right now, but they may later, and by then *you'll* be the expert. Besides, when you're home alone with the new baby, you may find yourself wishing for someone who can talk about something beyond formula and bowel movements. You might want to hear that there's still a world beyond motherhood.

Professional Care

Friends are great to listen to you, advise you (assuming they have some degree of competence), and provide that much-needed hug when you're down. But when you need more professional advice look to your doctors and nurses and the support people who are providing prenatal care. If you go to a clinic (that happens to be more affordable because it's less private), you may find yourself with a rotating shift of doctors. That makes it hard to

establish a relationship with your primary-care physician.
(Not all clinics operate that way, however. You may have
appointments with one specific doctor, but he or she may
not be the one who helps with your delivery.) If your
doctor does change with each appointment, try to establish rapport with the nurses. You need to feel comfortable with those who are taking care of you so that
you'll feel free to ask about whatever is bothering you.
Remember, they work for you even if they're paid from
government funds, and you're entitled to be taken
seriously and treated with respect.

Actually, I believe doctors like to have patients ask
questions or voice complaints. It's hard for them to guess
how a patient is feeling. Don't assume that because you're
younger than most patients, your questions or complaints
will be laughed off. No one will think you're being
"babyish" unless you act that way by whining or demanding special attention. Asking questions about your
condition, about labor and your ability to get through it,
is not whining.

Alternatives to Family Support

It's harder to deal with your pregnancy when you have
little or no family support, but alternatives are available.
Many community service agencies will provide you with
financial resources and prenatal care, or at least help you
obtain them. As mentioned in Chapter 1, most family
planning clinics offer free pregnancy testing. If you can't
afford to pay hospital and doctor bills, they'll help you file
the appropriate forms to get Title XIX benefits that *will*
pay those costs. It is easier to have these people steer
you through the paperwork than to wander through the

halls of Human Services trying to find the right person to file your claim. Family planning clinics offer referral services, which means they can point you in the right direction if they can't help you with what you need. They can help you find a support group for pregnant teenagers; they can help you find a childbirth class to join; they can help you find lodging (and the financial resources to pay for it).

Some clinics have emergency supplies of baby food and can lend you baby furniture, baby products, and maternity clothing. All the teenager has to do is show need and promise to return the things borrowed. Later on, these same support personnel can help with birth-control information and filing for welfare assistance.

The advantage of developing a relationship with someone at a clinic is that you have another human being willing to walk you through one of the most confusing times in your life. The staff member, who often has a background in counseling or health education, can provide short-term counseling or refer you to another professional should you need more intensive treatment for an emotional problem. He or she can offer you concrete resources, not merely advice, which is nice when you're already filled up with family members' words of wisdom. After the baby comes, you can continue at some clinics to receive baby-care education and birth-control information.

Most agencies (whether they're funded by a church or by private donations) prefer to work with teenagers who have told their parents. If this is difficult for you, they'll help you break the news. Some agencies will treat a teenager without parental awareness if the teenager believes she has been exposed to a sexually transmitted disease such as AIDS. However, if keeping your parents out of the picture is of concern to you, ask about policy before you involve yourself.

Planned Parenthood in most cases offers pregnancy testing, birth control information, and a prenatal clinic with a sliding-scale fee (which means you pay what you can afford to pay—determined by them, of course). Sometimes these clinics work with hospitals so that you see your doctor for prenatal visits at the clinic, and the same doctor delivers you in the hospital.

You can find family planning clinics in the Yellow Pages of your phone book under Birth Control, Family Planning, and Pregnancy Counseling. Planned Parenthood will be listed in the white pages if there's one in your area.

The city health department is an inexpensive alternative to family planning clinics, but the waiting list for treatment is usually long and the care provided less private.

Support from the School System

Another important support system you'll need is— believe it or not—your school. Maybe you're one of those students who feel misunderstood by teachers and only visit the guidance office to pick your courses for the upcoming year. Maybe getting pregnant was a rationalization for dropping out of school. I've already given you my lecture on staying in school, but I didn't say what kind of school to stay in. Until I started researching the subject, I didn't know so many alternatives to traditional school existed. You can check out what is available in your school district, but the least you'll probably be offered is a private tutor when you're too pregnant to go to class. Alternative school programs for pregnant and parenting teens number in the hundreds. Some programs allow the pregnant teenager to continue taking class with her peers but also to take health classes and parenting classes so that she'll be better prepared for parenthood. When the baby comes, she can resume classes and leave her infant in the capable hands of day-care workers next door to the school. For some girls the idea of never leaving their old school and friends is appealing, but for others it is intimidating. "I didn't want to hang around a place where everyone was staring at me all the time," one girl told me. "And I sure didn't want to try to squeeze myself into those desks, or have my water break in class, or something equally embarrassing."

Because many girls want to be "separate but equal" with their old schools, some programs take the teen out of the traditional setting and house the program in a separate facility. The teenager is surrounded by other pregnant and parenting teenagers, and the day-care facility is right at the school so the girls can be close to their babies. These programs help the teens learn to be good parents as well as good students. They learn (from their teachers as well as counselors and school nurses) how to take care of themselves and how to take care of a baby. More than that, the staff and students become close to one another, with the adults serving as mentors and giving the girls hugs and support that they might not be getting anywhere else. The teens I talked with in some of the programs actually looked forward to school each day. They discovered that school gave them more than education; it gave them back their self-esteem. They were learning to take care of themselves.

"Self-Support"

Last, but far from least, *you* are your own best support. First of all, take care of yourself. In the next chapter I'll discuss things *not* to do, but for now I'll just mention how you can start out caring for your health. Taking care of yourself benefits the baby as much as you. The baby receives its nourishment from you; what goes into you eventually gets to the baby. Think of that when you're about to tear into that bag of potato chips.

Doctors will prescribe vitamins for you, but vitamins are *supplements* to balanced meals, not meant to replace them. You need to eat vegetables, fruits, proteins, and dairy products. In fact, as a teenager you need to increase your protein intake and drink an extra glass of milk each day. If you're taking an iron supplement (as most doctors will prescribe), you're probably going to get constipated. Iron does that, and having your insides all squooshed out of place by your expanding uterus doesn't help either. You don't need laxatives; they can be dangerous, particularly as you approach labor. Eat more green, leafy vegetables and fresh fruit. Drink eight to ten glasses of water a day. You probably think you hit the bathroom enough as it is, but the water flushes out your system. It will not make you need to urinate much more often than you already do. If you have a real problem with constipation, try a natural-fiber preparation such as Metamucil or Fiberall. More words of wisdom: Limit your fat intake, lay off the junk food, and watch out for artificial sweeteners. Not that I know something bad about artificial sweeteners per se; but we don't know enough yet, so better play it safe than sorry.

Advice from Teen Moms

1. "Be careful and take care of yourself when you're eating for two."
2. "When you're pregnant, take care of yourself and eat right."
3. "By all means, don't drop out of school."
4. "Become involved with support groups and/or church activities. Sometimes they provide assistance at times of need."

CHAPTER 3

Feeling Like You're Crazy

When I was planning this book, I assumed that most of you teenagers would encounter a pregnancy only by accident. It hadn't occurred to me (until you mentioned it) that some of you might be married and *choose* to get pregnant now. So some parts of this book may not apply to you, or you'll have to adapt the message to your particular situation. However, this chapter is not one of them.

Everyone, and I include us old folks who had kids in our twenties and thirties, undergoes the physical changes of pregnancy. Some women handle the changes better than others, and most handle them better when they know what to expect—once they know they're not really going crazy.

This chapter will cover most of the physical side effects of pregnancy as well as possible emotional changes. Don't feel that you have to experience all of them in order to be "normal." There is no normal pregnancy that I know of.

I'll suggest ways to lessen the symptoms that bother you most, but in many circumstances it's a matter of simply hanging in there for the next several months. Knowing it'll be over then is as much as you can hope for. I'll also warn you about things to avoid when you're pregnant so that you remain healthy. And last will be some comments from other teen moms about the best and worst parts of pregnancy for them.

Nausea

The first physical change you'll probably notice is nausea. Many women get a queasy stomach early in pregnancy; some become violently ill and spend part of each day vomiting. Nausea doesn't indicate anything good or bad about your pregnancy, or whether you're carrying a boy or a girl. Some people get sick; others don't. Doctors say it more than likely has to do with the rise in hormones that sustains your pregnancy. Theoretically the nausea and vomiting last only three months, but some women report feeling sick around certain foods for the duration of the pregnancy.

If you're one of the unlucky ones who do get sick at the beginning of pregnancy, take heart. There are things you can do besides park yourself in the bathroom for three months. If you get sick upon rising in the morning (the typical time for nausea to set in), keep some crackers on your nightstand. Start nibbling the crackers before you even lift your head off the pillow. Eat several small meals throughout the day instead of three large meals at specific times. Consult your doctor or nurse if you simply can't keep food down. Remember, the baby gets nourishment from you, and if you're not getting anything substantial, neither is he (or she). If you can't eat anything, at least keep drinking. You don't want to dehydrate too. Popsicles are good to suck on because they're cold as well as tasty. Frozen fruit juice bars have some nutritional value too. And as I said, the nausea should pass in three months. Keep looking ahead.

One last thought: Don't *expect* to get sick. Not all women do. If you don't sit around expecting it, maybe it won't happen. When I had my children I always had trouble believing I was pregnant at first because I never got sick. I thought all pregnant women spent the first three months on the bathroom floor!

Fatigue

You'll probably start feeling more tired than usual, and as your pregnancy progresses you'll even want to take naps to get through the day. Resting more doesn't mean you're wimping out. You'll need your rest for several reasons. First, you're sustaining a life inside you, and your heart has to work harder. Second, you need to conserve some of your energy for labor. Third, toward the end of pregnancy you'll have trouble sleeping at night (that's the time when the fetus decides to play blocks inside you), and you'll fall asleep midway through the day anyway. If you're tired, sleep. If you can't stretch out, at least put your feet up. Just because you're young and athletic doesn't mean you can glide through pregnancy with only five hours of sleep a night. When your belly starts ballooning, it'll be hard to sleep in any position. Doctors suggest lying on your side, with a pillow propped between your legs for comfort. Don't lie flat on your back; that puts more strain on your insides.

You, and the whole world, will know that you spend the greater part of each day going to the bathroom. In the beginning you need to urinate more frequently because the bladder rests on the uterus, and your uterus is expanding. During the fifth, sixth, and seventh months it may not seem so bad, but actually you've just gotten used to going to the bathroom every hour or so. In the last stages of pregnancy you'll again feel you're going a lot. By then, your poor bladder is so crowded that it can't hold on to its full capacity, and you may even "leak" if you laugh too hard or drink too much. You can't change that, but you can accommodate it. Wear panty shields if you worry about accidents. Whenever I was pregnant I always located the bathrooms first no matter where I went, and plotted the quickest routes too.

The Pregnant Belly

Naturally, your belly is going to expand. It doesn't happen overnight. You'll first notice your clothes feeling tighter and the waistbands having no give. When I was pregnant with my first child (and didn't know what to expect), I hid behind my desk at work because I had to unbutton my pants in order to breathe. Maternity clothes were out of the question: I couldn't afford to start wearing them two months into the pregnancy; otherwise I'd have to buy both summer and winter outfits. Not many people can afford several seasons of maternity clothes. So adjust your buttons; wear over-sized shirts and wait until your belly refuses to fit into your pants. That day will come soon enough.

One day you'll stare in the mirror at this round mound that is your stomach. You'll first think you've put on weight, and you'll try to suck in your gut. But it won't move. When you touch it or press in on it, it'll be hard as a rock. Having worried about "getting fat" when I first became pregnant, this rock-hard belly sticking out of my clothes was almost more than I could stand. Suddenly I had lost control of my body, and it was blowing up right before my eyes.

Don't panic! You're young, and you can regain your shape quite easily. If you do have trouble with weight, check out Weight Watchers afterwards; you'll be surprised how fast the weight can come off if you watch what you eat.

Some women are proud of their growing bellies and actually feel more attractive. If you're one of them, you don't need any advice.

Other Symptoms

You may encounter some other symptoms that are all part and parcel of being pregnant. Hemorrhoids! Since you'll probably be constipated and have trouble with bowel movements, you may develop hemorrhoids too. You'll notice blood in your bowel movements, and it may hurt when you strain on the toilet. Don't get into the habit of using laxatives; you'll become dependent on them. Instead, eat more fruits and vegetables, or try a natural-fiber preparation as suggested in Chapter 2.

Doctors see more bladder infections in pregnant women. They say we don't drink enough fluids. So drink up, no matter how much you hate those filling, boring glasses of water.

You'll probably experience an increase in vaginal discharge. As long as it doesn't signal an infection (by odor or profusion), just learn to live with it. Toward the end of pregnancy the vaginal canal needs to be well lubricated for the baby. If it bothers you, wear panty shields.

You may experience sinus trouble, nosebleeds, and

headaches. Everything becomes congested when you're pregnant, including your sinuses. Take Tylenol as needed for pain, and rest. Don't get hooked on nasal spray. Doctors told me to use something called Ocean that you can buy in any drugstore. It didn't provide as much relief as nasal spray, but at least I didn't get hooked on it. With headaches, as long as you don't have blurry vision or nausea or sharp pain, just take Tylenol and relax. This too will pass.

Your skin will become itchy because it's drier. Just slather it with lotion and avoid long, hot baths. Stretch marks? If you get them (and not all women do; I never did in any of my pregnancies), keep applying lotion to them. The marks across your abdomen may look ugly, but after the baby is born they'll fade somewhat into pearly white lines. Having stretch marks does not mean you didn't take care of yourself or that you gained too much weight too fast. Actually it is related to genetics. Some people have more elastic skin than others. About all you can do is keep the skin lubricated—and cover up, if the lines offend you.

Along with a bigger belly come bigger breasts. Your breasts will enlarge because they are preparing to feed the baby. After nineteen weeks or so they'll start leaking colostrum in preparation for birth and afterwards. Don't worry; you won't start dripping milk all over your shirt. You'll probably be the only one who'll notice it in your bra.

You may experience leg cramps, particularly at night. If you've never felt a leg cramp, it's like having a hot wire stuck down the length of your side. To put it mildly, it hurts. Change position; take a warm bath. Tell your doctor if it happens often or lasts more than a few minutes.

You may feel dizzy when you stand up or get up in the morning. Remember, your heart is working overtime to take care of you and the fetus, so you need to rest more. Getting up alters your blood pressure; hence, dizziness. Try doing everything in slow motion. It helps.

As if we don't suffer enough assaults to our dignity in being pregnant, there's *gas*. Your stomach will churn, and your bowels will rumble. Passing gas is a relief when it's not an embarrassment. Because your intestines are being squooshed out of shape by your uterus, they have a harder time moving food along quietly. Before you take an over-the-counter drug for gas, check with your doctor.

Some women develop what's called "the mask of pregnancy." It's a dark patch over part of your face, which eventually subsides after childbirth. I never had that, but I did get a dark brown line down the middle of my abdomen, which made me look cut in half. That too disappears a few weeks or months after delivery.

Toward the end of pregnancy you may start feeling breathless as your uterus pushes against your diaphragm. Sometimes you can feel the baby's foot in your rib cage or kicking you in other unpleasant ways. One thing that really embarrassed me when wearing tight-fitting sweaters was noticing strange lumps moving across the breadth of my belly at odd times. It looked as if a mole had burrowed under my sweater, and it provided many entertaining moments for those who happened to catch sight of me.

You may notice something about your pregnancy that I haven't mentioned. It doesn't mean that you're abnormal, nor does it mean that it's not a problem. Anything that bothers you is worth mentioning to your doctor and nurse. The following paragraphs discuss symptoms that require *immediate* attention.

Serious Symptoms

A problem that requires prompt attention is vaginal bleeding, which could have a variety of causes. Not all bleeding is dangerous. Sometimes it occurs after sexual intercourse. Some women bleed around the time of their missing period for a couple of months. But any amount of steady bleeding should be reported to your doctor. It could be a sign of placental problems. If you have placenta previa, your placenta is lying low over your cervix, and you'll probably need a Cesarean section at delivery. (You can't deliver the placenta before the child.) Abruptio placenta is even more dangerous; it signifies that the placenta (or part of it) has broken away from the lining of the uterus.

If your water breaks, doctors will want to see you because of the risk of infection. Usually they will attempt to deliver the baby within twenty-four hours (unless the pregnancy is not far enough along for the fetus to survive).

Any dizziness coupled with blurry vision and headache can signify preeclampsia, eclampsia, or toxemia. Call your doctor right away. These are life-threatening conditions in the extreme. High blood pressure is common in teenagers under age seventeen. If pressure rises too high and is left untreated, it can lead to convulsions.

Any swelling (particularly any sudden swelling) in the limbs or continuous vomiting should be reported.

Special Considerations

Pregnancy does not mean an end to sex. You can have sexual relations all the way up to delivery if you're so inclined. But all teenagers should be responsible, and pregnant teens even more so. You must be certain of your partner's sexual history and of his fidelity. You can't tell by looking at a person whether he has a sexually transmitted disease (STD), even AIDS. If you engage in unprotected sex (just because you're already pregnant), be prepared for dire consequences unless you can vouch that your partner is "clean."

What STDs should you worry about? Herpes, for one. It's a common enough infection, but it can't be cured, only treated. You don't get rid of herpes; it merely goes into remission from time to time. If you have an active case of herpes when you go into labor, you'll need to have a Cesarean section to avoid passing on the infection (and other risks) to the baby as it moves through the birth canal.

Women are tested for gonorrhea with all the other blood tests during prenatal care. However, you can always catch gonorrhea, and ninety-eight percent of women show no symptoms.

Chlamydia is the most common STD in the United States today. The only symptom may be an increase in vaginal discharge. Chlamydia can be passed to the baby in the birth canal, resulting in eye infection, pneumonia, and stomach and intestinal problems. Chlamydia is easily treated with erythromycin, a drug that is not known to be harmful to the fetus.

If you have reason to believe you've been exposed to AIDS, tell the doctor immediately. Get yourself tested; some doctors ask you to have an AIDS test anyway when you're pregnant. Not having a test won't make the HIV virus go away; it will be there whether you face up to it or not. And don't take the foolish attitude that it couldn't happen to you. It can happen to anyone. Just consider Magic Johnson . . .

AIDS has no cure so far. If you have it, more than likely your baby will be born with it.

Emotional Aspects of Pregnancy

So far, I've concentrated on the physical aspects of pregnancy. Sometimes more difficult to deal with are the emotional aspects. The emotional ups and downs are a reflection of your raging hormones, your attitude toward the event, and how much support you have. Being upset doesn't mean that you're a bad person or that you reject the pregnancy. Anyone is bound to feel stressed by such an important event. But being stressed (both physically and mentally) makes one more apt to fly off the handle. So let's look at all the ways you might be feeling without judging what kind of a person that makes you.

Some people feel only joy and happiness during pregnancy. Every discomfort is welcomed because it reminds the woman that she's actually having a baby. Maybe you're excited because you are soon to be a mother. You'll have a cuddly little baby to love and who'll love you back. (Later we'll look at the fallacy of that idea, but for now let's just accept it as the way some teens feel at this point.) Some teens feel more loved, more creative, and more important. If you feel that way you're lucky, because so positive an attitude will make it easier to handle all the bad parts of being pregnant.

But for the majority of women (teens and adults alike), pregnancy is a time when you just can't stay on top of your feelings. They simply change too often. One minute you're happy, the next minute you're worried. One day you're proud of your shape, the next day you're embarrassed. One day you appreciate your boyfriend's or your husband's concern, the next day you feel as if he takes no interest in you.

Accept all your feelings, even the negative ones. Being upset and angry at your circumstances isn't unusual and doesn't mean you're hurting the baby. Hating the pregnancy doesn't mean you hate the child you've created. Pregnancy is hard work, no doubt about it. If your boyfriend or husband disputes that, tie a twenty-pound sack of potatoes to his belly and let him walk around all day struggling to support it. I'll bet it'll destroy his humor as much as his lower back.

At some point you're going to realize that, "Oh, my gosh! I'm going to have to go through with this." That's when you'll really need a support system in place: someone who will listen to you complain, who will give you comfort and assurance that you'll do just fine.

You may be scared about the actual process of childbirth. We're all scared of the unknown. I had my first child at the ancient age of twenty-nine, but I was terrified nonetheless. When I was only three months pregnant, my husband found me sitting in the bathroom crying my eyes out. I didn't think I could actually bear the baby, and I knew there was no way back. One way or another, the baby was going to be born. I was afraid because I didn't know how much it would hurt and whether or not I could stand the pain. Did people still die in childbirth?

Men have a hard time understanding our fears, for one thing because they never have to go through the experience. But men prefer to solve problems rather than listen to women complain, so don't be surprised if your boyfriend or husband reacts with dismay that you're worried about something you can do nothing to change. What helped me was talking with others (mostly other pregnant women, but also nurses and other professionals) about the process of birth and what options I had for pain relief. For that very reason, I've included a chapter on labor and delivery, and I suggest you read Chapter 5 before you find yourself in the throes of labor pains and hospital procedures. The more you know ahead of time, the less you have to fear.

You may feel more dependent and "babyish" around your boyfriend, husband, or mother. When you're vulnerable you do tend to become more dependent. Accept it for now; you'll revert to your usual nature after delivery.

You may worry whether the baby is going to be okay. I'll talk in a moment about dangers in the environment, but aside from them, staying healthy yourself will ensure a healthy baby. Share your concerns with your health care providers, however; they'll tell you that you're not the first person to worry about that, and in most cases everything is absolutely fine.

You'll no doubt be excited when you first feel the baby move—and every time the baby moves, although the experience loses its charm when feet start poking you in the rib cage. The baby is always moving, but you'll become aware of the fluttery feelings around the fifth or sixth month. At first it may feel like indigestion or bubbles bursting inside you. You may even get used to the sensations and miss them after delivery.

It's important to stay healthy, not only to make for an easier delivery for you, but to ensure a healthy baby. Whatever you ingest crosses the placenta to the fetus. That's why you need to stay away from drugs and alcohol. Even if you drink only a small amount of beer or wine, the fetus ends up with the same proportion in its body. Your liver can process the alcohol out of your system, but the fetus's immature liver is not capable of doing so. Babies born with fetal alcohol syndrome (because their mothers drank too much while pregnant) can have neurological problems that affect their intelligence, motor abilities, coordination, and judgment. Fetal alcohol syndrome is not reversible. If you doubt that it's a serious problem, read the excellent book by Michael Dorris, *The Broken Cord*, about his son's struggles because of it.

The U.S. Food and Drug Administration states, "Presently, there is no known safe level of alcohol consumption below which no risk is present." That means that no one knows how little one can drink and still permanently damage her child. Why take any risk at all?

Drug abuse (and who knows how much use constitutes abuse?) can lead to low-birth-weight babies. It can cause premature separation of the placenta, resulting in a stillbirth and the mother's possible bleeding to death. In thirty-eight percent of pregnancies in which the mother abuses drugs, miscarriage results. A large number go into premature labor. It doesn't particularly matter which drug you abuse; they all carry consequences. Crack cocaine quickly causes addiction, however. Because it is smoked, the cocaine reaches the brain faster and in greater quantity. Crack causes an increase in blood pressure. Remember, your heart is already working doubly hard to maintain a normal pregnancy. The stress from high blood pressure compounds that.

Cocaine addiction can lead to respiratory and kidney disease in the fetus. The baby will be born with a lack of muscle coordination. He himself may be addicted to the drug and will be crankier than normal and underweight. Because of all that, he'll also be at greater risk of developing sudden infant death syndrome (SIDS).

Is it really that important to you to risk your baby's health (not to mention your own) for a few moments of euphoria? If you're already addicted, get into a substance-abuse program. Drug-addicted mothers are not good mothers. They can't be, because they're always working on getting the next fix. If you're not a good mother, you stand to lose your child. If you don't know of a drug-abuse program in your area, call the drug hotline: 1-800-662-HELP. This is a free call for referral to a drug-treatment program and is operated by the National Institute on Drug Abuse.

Of course, you've heard about the dangers of smoking, whether you're pregnant or not. Cigarettes contain 4,000 chemicals that will cross the placenta. When you light up and inhale, the fetus suddenly gets less oxygen. If you smoke regularly, the fetus can suffer from low birth weight, prematurity, or stillbirth. Smoking is an addiction, believe it or not, so you may need help in quitting.

Secondhand smoke is equally dangerous to your unborn child. You get just as many chemicals when you breathe in the smoke other people exhale. Stay out of smoke-filled rooms, and get others to refrain from smoking around you. If you find it hard to ask people to quit, consider the life of your unborn child.

Other dangers in the environment include smog (not much you can do if you live in the wrong city, except stay indoors), and lead paint. If you live in an older place, don't scrape the paint or refinish furniture when you're pregnant. And don't hang around while others are doing it. Don't expose yourself to fumes like cleaning fluid, glue, or pesticides. Wash all vegetables and fruits carefully. Avoid aerosol products; switch to pump containers. If you have a cat, don't handle its box either. Cats can carry a disease called toxoplasmosis, which can cause retardation and other neurological problems in your unborn baby. Better leave the changing of the box to someone else in the family.

Advice from Teen Moms

"Stay away from drugs. They may make you feel better when things are going bad, but all that does is repress the feelings until a later date. Not only that, it's a waste of money."

The best thing about being pregnant was . . .

- "knowing the wonderful time I'll have with my child."
- "that very second when he got here."
- "having my boyfriend there."
- "getting attention."
- "having a baby that I can love."
- "not having a period."
- "when it was over."
- "feeling like I was loved."
- "at the end, getting a beautiful child."
- "feeling the baby move and the anticipation of seeing your baby."

The worst thing about being pregnant was . . .

- "starting to dislike foods I used to love and eating foods that I used to hate."
- "hating to listen to music."
- "being so fat."
- "the many mood changes."
- "having a blemish on my face."
- "feeling fat and ugly and that I'll never have this kid."
- "gaining almost 80 pounds."

- "not being able to fit into any of my clothes."
- "always feeling sick and tired and dizzy."
- "always being in a grouchy mood."
- "not being able to smoke or have as much coffee as I wanted."
- "when the baby's father left me for another girl."
- "getting fat."
- "getting sick."
- "feeling miserable all the time."
- "being scared of what's to come and not being able to get a part-time job. No one will hire a pregnant person."

CHAPTER 4

How Will You Keep This Child?

O f course, you *want* this child, but providing for the child is a whole other matter. Most first-time parents know very little about how much money it will cost to feed, clothe, and care for this new little creature. And those of you who've never been on your own know equally little about providing for yourself. So in this chapter we'll look at the costs involved in preparing for the baby as well as the considerations for housing and support. If you already think your situation is beyond hope, cheer up. There are always alternatives to having rich parents.

Before you can even think about how you're going to buy all that basic baby equipment, you need to know how you're going to live and feed yourself first. Maybe your options will already be reduced by the time your parents find out about your pregnancy. Maybe they'll flatly tell you that you can't live with them and expect their support. Maybe your home life is so chaotic that you wouldn't want to live under their roof even if they offered it. But more than likely, particularly if you're a young teenager (or not involved in a steady relationship), you'll stay with your parents.

Living at Home

Living with your parents can be good for two reasons. One, you don't have to pay room and board (which costs an arm and a leg out in the real world), and two, you have some ready-made company. Once the baby comes, you'll have to sit down with your folks and decide just what everyone's role will be. You're an adult now, remember? If you want them to be the baby's grandparents, don't expect them to take on parental responsibilities as well. *You* change the diapers, orchestrate the feedings, and arrange for sitters. It isn't particularly rewarding work, and it's certainly not the fun part of raising a child, but then, you're the mother, right? Don't assume that your mother is always free and willing to watch the baby so you can go out with your friends. (I told you there's a downside to being an adult, and this happens to be part of it.)

Then again, if you're not able to take responsibility for the baby, your parents may have to take over for you. If you abdicate your mothering role to them, don't complain when the baby looks to them as parents. If you count on them to provide the day-to-day care of the baby, don't complain when they provide the discipline too.

Whose Support?

Perhaps you just don't want to be dependent on your parents any longer. Or maybe you think it'll be easier to live on your own, making the rules and enforcing them as you choose. First of all, let's dispel some myths. Living on your own is not necessarily easier. You have to have a decent place to live, and decent places cost money. How will you afford such a place? If you're working (and if you've dropped out of high school, you probably have only a minimum-wage job at best), how long will you be able to work? What will happen when you take time off to have the baby? What will happen even later when you need a baby-sitter, or when the baby is too sick to go to day care and you have used up all your sick leave? Welfare is no substitute for wages; it simply is not enough to pay for a good place to live and leave enough to buy groceries too.

So your first consideration will be: *How will I support myself?* Will you struggle on your own, or will you find a roommate? Will that roommate be someone equally responsible, or someone who is also looking to get away from home? If you move in with your boyfriend, will he quit school to get a job? Will he take care of you, or resent you for making him become an adult too soon? Should you marry him now, wait until you see what kind of father he'll make, or live freely so you can separate more easily if the time comes?

Ethnic Differences

What if your boyfriend is black and you are white? What if only one of you is Hispanic or Indian? Does that even matter? Girls tell me it does matter when a baby is involved. You and the baby's father may be able to handle your different skin colors, but chances are your parents will have a tougher time doing so. Your baby will be a mixture, and consequently not the same as either of you. If you are white, how will your darker-skinned baby be

treated by your parents or your neighbors? Will it matter
to you? Or will you find yourself explaining why you with
your free-swinging blonde hair have a baby with olive-
colored skin and kinky black hair? And if you and your
boyfriend break up, will another guy accept this child?

Our country may be integrated, but its social tolerance
has not dramatically increased. As a teenager, you may
not care what other people think of you and whom you
date. Perhaps that's part of the appeal of dating someone
not of your race; it flies into the teeth of the rules. But
when you have a child, at some point you'll have to
consider the impact on him or her. He or she will *always*
have to deal with having one parent of one color and the
other of a different color.

Don't misunderstand me; I'm not saying that these
relationships won't last or are not good. I'm simply warn-
ing you of the pressures and conflicts that lie ahead.
Forewarned, one is better defended. Expect your parents
to treat the baby as the lovable grandchild that he or she
will be no matter what color his skin. If they can't accept
the child (or his father), stay away until you can figure the
best way to get along. You don't want your child to incor-
porate their rejection into his self-image.

The Baby's Father

Getting along with your boyfriend (whether you make
him your husband or not) is hard work anyway, even if
you're of the same race, religion, and social class. It will
be hard for a guy to understand your needs right now.
(I'm not saying that to excuse the guy from trying to
understand you. It is generally accepted that guys don't
readily understand things outside of their experience,
and bearing children is not part of their experience.)

Your boyfriend may be preoccupied with his upcoming responsibilities. He may be angry at having to give up some things for you (maybe his dream of a career or travel). If he's honest, he may admit to jealousy over the attention you're getting. My husband struggled with fears about being a good-enough father: Was he up to the task? Would he do a better job than his father did with him? I didn't worry about being a good-enough mother; I didn't have time for that. I was too worried about whether I was going to survive labor or make a fool of myself in the delivery room.

Keep the communication lines open with your boy-friend/spouse. In the beginning the pregnancy will be more important to you, mostly because it will be apparent only to you. In the first trimester (the first three months of pregnancy), you'll believe in it because you're the one feeling all those hormonal changes. The guy can't readily *see* that you're carrying a child, so it's not as apparent to him. Not that he doesn't believe in it per se; he just doesn't acknowledge it. The fetus is not a physical reality to him at this point. Along about the time you're more comfortable with yourself (in the second trimester), your boyfriend will start to see for himself that you're pregnant. Then he may start being extra careful with you—although by that time you won't feel so fragile. After all, you've felt this pregnancy for three whole months already.

So the pregnancy experience may widen the gap between males and females. If you share with him your feelings, fears, and hopes, you'll make the experience more significant to him. But do him the same courtesy. Listen to him, and encourage him to talk about what's happening inside him. When people listen to each other without passing judgment, they validate each other. You'll be saying to each other, "How you're feeling right now is important to me." Just remind the guy from time to time (as I have to with my husband) that he doesn't have to *solve* all your problems. Usually, it's enough simply to listen.

If you don't have parental support, and your boyfriend has flown the coop, you may have to live by yourself. Unless you're an exceptionally mature teenager or have already been living on your own, consider this option a last resort. It is hard to support yourself on your own, but more than that, it's lonely. Are you afraid of the dark? Do you have trouble staying off the telephone when you're all by yourself? How will you even furnish the place? One girl I taught told me proudly of the new apartment she was moving into that week.

"What's it like?" I asked.

"Well, it's brand-new and has shag carpeting and everything," she said.

"Is it furnished?" I asked.

"No, but I'm going to get some stuff myself," she said.

Turned out the only things she brought with her from her parent's apartment were her bed and dresser. Empty rooms can be depressing, not to mention inconvenient. It costs a lot to furnish a place—to buy a table and chairs, a sofa, bed, and dresser—so think before you just decide to move out.

Needs and Wants for the Baby

Now let's look at what the baby will need. Don't get discouraged yet. If you can't afford to buy all the basics new—and not many teenage parents can—I'll tell you other ways (short of stealing) to get them.

First of all, learn how to draw up a budget and then stay within it. One of the hardest things for anyone to learn (and I'm still working on it myself) is to live within your means. What distinguishes kids from adults (no matter what the ages) is that kids can't wait to get what they want. Adults learn to delay gratification, that is, to wait until they an afford to get something, no matter how much they want it *right then*! Figure out how much money will come in regularly and decide what things (rent, utilities, food) must be paid first. Allocate the remaining money wisely. Ask a capable adult (your parents, a counselor, or a teacher) to help you prepare a budget if you have no experience.

I then tell girls I've counseled to draw up a list of wants and needs for the baby. What are the items you want for the baby, and what are the items you *must* have to provide proper care. Take care of the *needs* first, then tackle the *wants* with any leftover money.

What should you buy new? A mattress and an infant car seat. (That doesn't mean *you* have to buy them; maybe your parents or grandparents will.)

You should buy a new mattress because they break down so easily from use. You'll have to have a car seat just to get your baby out of the hospital. Most places will not let you take the baby home without your first producing the car seat. One reason to buy it new is that car seats are being improved constantly; what was acceptable a year or two ago may no longer pass muster. Also, the newer ones are easier to use. What's the point of putting your baby in a car seat and then leaving the buckles undone because they're too much trouble? The older models have about twenty buckles to mess with, whereas the newer ones have only one or two.

You can buy a crib at a secondhand store or garage sale, making sure the bars of the crib are no more than two to three inches apart. Disasters have happened when babies have forced heads between crib bars and been unable to get back.

You'll need a high chair eventually, and you may want a swing, playpen, or walker. If you can't afford these items yourself, see if you can borrow them from a friend or relative. Check with family planning clinics whether they lend baby furniture. Visit garage sales or consignment shops for bargains. Since baby stuff is used only for a few years, most things should be in good condition.

What you can't buy yourself or your parents can't afford, look for secondhand. Make a list of things you need. Then if a friend decides to give you a shower or asks what you need for the baby, you can consult your list and tell him. Now is not the time to play coy and say, "Oh, get me anything." Do your friend and yourself a favor by being specific. People would rather give you something you need than something they think you need.

Baby Clothes

What besides furniture will the baby need? Depending on whether the baby is born in summer or winter, you can get away with a minimum of baby clothes. You'll need T-shirts and sleepers—lots of them; you'll be surprised how quickly a little teeny baby can soak its clothes. My son was adept at soaking his T-shirt without ever getting his diaper wet. (It's not too tricky, if you think about it.) You might prefer gowns with drawstrings at the bottom. They allow you to get at the baby's messy diaper more easily than fumbling with zippers and snaps in a sleeper. Have a lightweight jacket on hand, and a winter coverup if it's that time of year. These clothes you can borrow or buy secondhand. The only people you impress with designer labels at this point are your friends. The baby doesn't know the difference.

Have a lot of blankets and sheets on hand. It's amazing how many times you'll have to change the sheets in the first few days and weeks. Let's hope you can do your laundry at home; with all you'll be accumulating, you'd be hanging out around the clock at a launderette. That explains the appeal of disposable diapers. Cloth diapers you pay for once, but you have to wash and fold them endlessly. You can throw away the paper ones but you'll spend a fortune buying them, whether you opt for the store brand or buy the cute character-printed ones with extra padding in the front for boys. You buy what you can afford, and to help you keep things in perspective, remember what function the diaper serves: It collects messes; it's not a collector's item.

Toys

What about toys for the baby? At this point, you and your buddies will be more intrigued with the toys than the baby will. A mobile hung well above the crib out of reach is nice to have, as are gadgets that play lullabies to the baby. Beyond that, the baby won't be interested. It prefers the sight of your face and the sound of your voice to anything else. Remember, in the beginning the baby will be eating and sleeping, and that's about it.

If you have extra money, or have parents who simply can't resist, buy rattles and other brightly colored shake toys—things that the baby can explore (safely) with its mouth and hands later on. If you get stuffed animals, remember your baby's size. Don't dwarf him or her with an animal that appeals to you; get something small. Don't leave things in the crib that can suffocate the baby—

which means pillows! Babies sleep flat; they don't need pillows. Newborns cannot breathe through the mouth (or don't know that they can), so if they press their nose up against something they are not able to breathe.

Last, though certainly not least, line up a pediatrician for your baby and plan to visit him or her regularly. You don't go to the doctor only when you think the baby is sick. You get it all the shots, and you make sure you follow instructions about feeding and handling. The baby stays healthy because of these regular appointments. Keep them. If you can't afford a private pediatrician, consider taking your baby to the county health department for visits.

If you don't breast-feed your baby (more about that in a later chapter), you'll need to know what formula your doctor recommends. (Babies have different needs, and different formulas are available to meet those needs.) You can buy formula in powder form or premixed liquid. This is one place where you cannot skimp on quality. Diluting the formula with water to make it go further destroys its nutritional value. In effect you'll be starving your baby. Plan on spending a bundle of money on formula for at least the first year of your baby's life. If you're low on funds, ask for help from the welfare office, a family planning clinic, or your parents.

Keep revising your list and your budget. Your needs and wants will change periodically, and maybe your assets will grow as well.

Advice from Teen Moms

1. "Make the best life for your child, because you can never go back and change the way you raised your kid."

2. "Don't marry. If you have decent parents, let them help. If not, find help."
3. "Be prepared; your life will change. You must grow up. If you're not ready, let someone else raise the child."

CHAPTER 5

Curtain Time:

Are You Ready?

L abor and delivery will happen whether you're prepared or not. Eventually this baby is going to be born, and though we might want to skip this part of the event, that option isn't open to us. (Many were the moments during labor when I wanted to say to my husband, "Here, *you* take over now." But obviously it doesn't work that way . . .)

For some people (teens included), labor is a breeze, lasting a mere couple of hours. But for the majority of women labor lasts longer and is considerably more painful than menstrual cramps. (Whoever said a contraction is just a cramp, only stronger?) Part of what's so scary about it (and hence, makes it seem to hurt all the more) is that most teenagers don't know what to expect. Misunderstandings, confusion, and fear all contribute to a more painful experience than necessary. With that in mind, let's see what happens during childbirth and what you can do to make it less painful. Just as all pregnancies are different, so are all labors. You may not encounter the degree of pain I did, or you may experience symptoms I haven't noted here. This chapter is only meant to familiarize you with the process and a few of the possible complications.

Childbirth Classes

Obviously, I don't know all there is to know about childbirth. After you have read this chapter, I suggest you check out one of the childbirth books in the list of books For Further Reading. You can't know too much about labor and delivery. If you can afford it or know of free classes, take a childbirth class, whether or not you want to have an unmedicated delivery. You don't have to be married to take childbirth classes. Your mother or your best friend can be your support person. I know some teachers who have served as girls' labor coaches. And you're not committing yourself to natural childbirth just by joining the class. Many women (and men, too) simply want to know more about what's coming up.

If you can't take classes, you can still talk to your doctor, nurse, and school counselors about labor and delivery. You want to know what is available for pain relief before you're lying on the delivery table and swearing you're going to die. School counselors may not all be versed in health care procedures, but anyone who has ever gone through labor and delivery will remember it, believe me. They can either give you advice or suggest people and books that can.

Practice relaxation techniques ahead of time. You don't wait until your contractions are three minutes apart before you try to remember the techniques you learned in class. (If you don't know any relaxation techniques, we'll describe some midway through this chapter.)

Pain Medication

Before we look at the process of childbirth, let's consider what kind of medication is available to take care of the pain. Knowing there is relief makes the experience more manageable—or at least, it did for me.

First are the *painkillers* (like Demerol) that are used simply to ease the pain. The problem is that you can't have enough of the stuff to take away *all* the pain because the medication crosses the placenta, and you don't want the baby to get too much. Talk about this option with your doctor (or preferably someone who has used it before), if it interests you. I found that no amount of Demerol disguised the pain for me. It still hurt like crazy, and the drug made my brain so fuzzy that I wasn't certain if I'd had the baby or was still in labor. I could tell what was going on around me, but my mind was very foggy, and I kept insisting to the nurses that it was time for my next dose. Sometimes doctors use *tranquilizers* to relax you, so that you can help more with the delivery. I found that Valium doesn't do a heck of a lot in the final stages of labor. Relaxed or not, it all hurt!

Anesthetics are used to numb parts of your body so that you don't feel pain. An *epidural block* works by blocking sensation from your waist down. The anesthesiologist inserts the anesthetic into membranes surrounding the spinal canal in your lower back. The good part is that you have no awareness of pain and no dead feeling in your legs. It's as if the shot took away the pain and you can actually begin to enjoy the experience. The bad part is that the shot is hard to administer, so a qualified anesthesiologist must be on duty when you need it. Not only that, the shot itself is quite painful. The needle is long, and you have to curl up in a fetal position (which is probably the last thing you feel like doing at that point) so it can be inserted. Sometimes the anesthetic takes effect on only one side of your body, and you end up feeling one-sided contractions. I've had both good and bad experiences with the epidural block. Once I felt as if I were having a baby out of one side of my body. The other time I couldn't believe the relief I felt.

The *spinal block* is a shot similar to the epidural, but it can't be given until you're completely dilated. It too completely stops the pain, but as far as I'm concerned you've done all the work by then. Dilating is what hurts the most. Another drawback to the spinal block is the accompanying feeling of dead weight. My legs no longer seemed to belong to me, and I couldn't help push the baby out because I wasn't aware of any sensation to push. With a spinal block you have to stay flat on your back for twenty-four hours afterward to avoid the excruciating headache that comes from getting up before the anesthetic has worn off.

The *pudendal block* is an anesthetic given to numb the perineum for an episiotomy. The doctor gives you a quick shot (not particularly painful, though it's all relative to the greater pain of childbirth) to numb the area between the birth canal and the rectum. Then he makes a cut to widen the area for the baby to come out. It isn't as gross as it sounds. If tearing is occurring you'll feel a burning sensation, and you'll end up with a wound that's harder to sew up. Better to have the episiotomy if needed, and the shot isn't bad.

Your last resort (one that is not routine for regular

childbirth) is *general anesthesia,* in which the anesthesiologist puts you to sleep. At some point during a painful
labor experience you might think "going to sleep" is a
good idea, but it's not an option. It's only for surgery,
which we'll discuss at the end of the chapter.

Labor

Let's go back now and talk about what happens in labor
and why teenage pregnancies are considered high-risk
situations. Many complications can accompany teen pregnancy. If the adolescent hasn't finished her own growing,
her pelvis may be too small for a vaginal delivery. Cesarean
delivery (informally called C-section) is always more of a
risk because it is major surgery. Teens are often poorly
nourished, because they lack either the money or the
knowledge to eat better. They don't always seek early
prenatal care (because they're trying to keep the pregnancy a secret from their parents, or they don't know how
to pay for it), and part of what makes for an easy delivery
is a healthy pregnancy. Finally, adolescents risk developing toxemia in pregnancy from high blood pressure.

What actually happens in labor? The uterus contracts
to signal the beginning of birth. The cervix, which has
been closed during the pregnancy (to keep infection out
and the baby in), begins to open up. It will stretch to
10 centimeters in width, which is just enough in most
instances to allow safe passage of the baby's head, the
widest part of the baby. Normally in a first pregnancy it
takes sixteen hours for the baby to be born.

Your first indication that labor is about to begin may
be the loss of the mucous plug that has been in your
cervix all this time. You may notice blood or a heavy
vaginal discharge in your underwear, unrelated to any

pain. Labor will usually start within the day or week.

Contractions are best described as waves of pain, a tightening sensation in your abdomen that may eventually extend around to your lower back. Some people describe it as severe menstrual cramps, but it's worse than any menstrual cramps I've ever experienced. By the time the contractions are coming every other minute, you might swear you're in the grip of some horrible vise that never totally relinquishes its hold. Supposedly the contractions are rhythmical, but I couldn't get in touch with any rhythm myself.

If you don't hurt very much (and you won't in the early stages), relax. Maybe you'll be one of the lucky ones who never feel much pain during labor. If you do start hurting and are surprised at the intensity of the pain, remember those relaxation techniques you learned. Now's the time to start using them. If you don't have any, here are a few suggestions of my own, developed from my first unmedicated childbirth, which lasted twenty-six hours.

1. Have a focal point that you can take to the hospital with you, something that you can focus on to help overcome the pain. If you don't want to look at something, use a person's voice as your focal point.
2. During pregnancy, and well before labor, practice tightening isolated parts of your body. Start with your hands.
3. Tighten your hand into a fist. Hold for five seconds, then relax slowly.
4. Feel your hand go limp and your fist loosen. Wiggle your fingers to ensure that they're totally relaxed.
5. Move on to your arm. Follow the same pro-

cedure. Tighten the arm, hold the position for five seconds, and then release. What you are doing is learning how feels to relax your body. When you start having a contraction during labor, you'll naturally tighten up. If you know how "tension and tightness" feel, you can relax your body, letting go some of the pain that comes from tension.

6. Continue to tighten and relax each part of your body from your head to your toes.

7. During labor, have your support person help you relax when the pain is most intense by encouraging you to visualize specific tranquil scenes, such as a day in the sun at the beach, or a cooling mountain breeze. (Visualization doesn't require that you've been to these places, just that you can imagine them.)

8. When all else fails, focus on your partner's voice. Go beyond the words. Listen to the tone of his voice, listen to how it rises and falls. (If your partner can't keep his own anxiety out of his voice, focus on something else.)

9. Block out everything else. Shut your eyes and listen to your partner's voice, or the nurse's voice (if that's with whom you've bonded).

10. The pain will increase and become more frequent, but you can ride it out. Pain medication is always available, and you are not a failure for using it.

Let's look at some of the things that can happen during labor. When you're well into labor and the doctor says to head for the hospital, what types of procedure will you encounter?

While some hospitals no longer give enemas routinely, don't protest if you're offered one. You get constipated during pregnancy, and you might be surprised at what you've stored up prior to labor. Would you rather empty your bowels in the bathroom or a bedpan, or on the delivery room table? When you reach the stage where you're pushing the baby out, if your bowels are not empty, the contents will pass out along with the baby.

You'll have your pulse and blood pressure checked, your temperature taken—all the ordinary vital signs. If you're in the middle of a contraction, you'll probably resent the nurses probing you so. You may be hooked up to an IV so that liquids can be administered during labor. Dehydration is a complication, so doctors routinely request IVs to prevent it. If you don't want the IV, talk with your doctor about it ahead of time. You won't be in much of a position to argue about anything when you're in the midst of contractions. They'll probably hook up at least an external fetal monitor (a belt around your belly) to keep track of the baby during labor. The doctor may use an internal monitor, a little electrode inserted through your vagina and attached to the baby's scalp to check its heart rate. If you're not hooked up to monitors yet, you'll probably be encouraged to walk around. You may want to pace out of excitement or anxiety—or you may find the idea of walking revolting.

Stages of Birth

Stage 1 of childbirth includes the whole dilation process from 0 to 10 centimeters, roughly four fingers' width. Contractions occur every five minutes or so down to every two minutes, and they may last a full minute. Take the pains one at a time. Don't think about riding out several hours of them; that will discourage you. In the beginning, from 1 to 4 centimeters, it won't necessarily seem so bad. I remember telling my nurse, "This isn't so bad. I thought it was supposed to hurt."

"Don't worry, it'll hurt," she advised me.

Transition is the time (from 8 to 10 centimeters) when it really hurts. You may feel like vomiting, you may actually vomit, and you may experience uncontrollable shaking and chills. My legs shook so the first time that it scared my husband. It didn't bother me except that I couldn't control it. Transition fortunately is usually brief—well, compared to the rest of it. If you're still unmedicated, you may find yourself in a very ugly mood. I remember telling my husband I was sick of the whole thing and would he please just take me home! Toward the end you'll feel a pressure on your rectum and swear you need to move your bowels. It will be the baby, who has moved down into the birth canal and whose head is pressing against your rectum.

By this stage you will probably have lost all dignity. I didn't care how obnoxiously I acted to either my husband or the nurse; I was infuriated that they couldn't take this pain away. (In subsequent labors I used medication and did not experience these mood swings—probably because I wasn't hurting.) Anyway, transition is over when you're fully dilated, and there's nothing sweeter than hearing the nurse or doctor announce that you're "complete." (They will have been checking your progress, by measuring finger widths in your cervix, throughout your labor. You'll be relieved to have the hand probes end for the moment.)

Stage 2 signals pushing and delivery of the baby. It could last an hour or more, and while some people complain that the pushing hurt, I found the experience a blessed relief after contractions. It took a lot of energy to push and not push when the nurse told me, so maybe I was too busy to realize I was hurting, but I truly did not sense pain. (I got a sore throat, though, from all the heaving I did.) I suppose if this stage of labor goes on too long, you'll feel worn out, but usually it is a welcome part of delivery because it means the baby is about to be born. If you haven't been moved to the delivery room, you will be now.

Surprisingly, when the baby pops out (and that's how it seems), you'll feel immense relief. In a normal delivery the head comes out first, then the shoulders are maneuvered out, and the rest slips out like a fish. The pain is *gone*. There is no residual pain.

Stage 3 consists of the delivery of the placenta. It doesn't hurt, but it might be uncomfortable having the doctor press down on your belly or use instruments to extract it.

Support Person

During this whole process you need a support person to help you stay focused and calm. Whoever is there to help you (whether it's your mother or girlfriend or husband), be sure that person is there for *you*, not to chat with the nurses. Make sure the support person realizes that you may behave badly during labor and say things you don't mean. I threw up on my husband during labor. He just peeled off his sweater and continued to sit by me and talk to me calmly.

The nurse who helps you through labor won't be the nurse you got to know in your doctor's office. He or she is someone who works solely in the labor and delivery room. The experience of your contractions depends to some extent on your relationship to this person. Can you bond with this nurse? Is she responsive to you? Does a shift change occur during your labor so that midway through you get a new nurse? Teens told me they did better in labor if they liked the nurse and were willing to follow her advice.

Cesarean Section

What about a C-section? The doctor may consider a C-section (which is making an incision in your abdomen to get at the baby) for several reasons. One is if you are in labor for hours without dilating and artificial stimulation (with pitocin, for example) doesn't help. Another reason is if the baby is in a breech position (with buttocks presenting first instead of head) or any other unusual position and can't be turned. It is much more painful (and risky to the baby) to deal with a breech delivery. You may also have a C-section if you have blood pressure problems or your water has broken more than twenty-four hours earlier.

If during labor, you pass meconium-stained water, it means that the baby has had a bowel movement in utero. It is at risk of swallowing the liquid if not delivered immediately. Allowing the fetus's lungs to fill with meconium-stained water risks infection and respiratory problems. The monitors can indicate any fetal distress during labor (reflected in a reduced heart rate). If there is distress that cannot be corrected, the doctor will perform an emergency C-section.

When you're going through labor and feeling awful, you might think a C-section would be a lot easier, particularly if you were put to sleep for it. But a C-section is major surgery, and it's not used as an alternative to a painful vaginal delivery. Recovery is longer and more painful, and you'll be glad later that you didn't have one.

You may be awake or asleep during a Cesarean delivery. If there is time to administer anesthetic, you'll be numbed and left alert to watch (behind the draped sheets) the birth of your baby. Your support person will be allowed in the room only if it has been agreed upon in advance and his (or her) being there won't interfere with the surgery. If it's an emergency procedure (or the epidural block isn't totally effective), you'll be given general anesthesia. Your support person, husband or not, may be barred from surgery under those circumstances. Hospitals and doctors differ on the matter. The surgery takes about an hour. The baby is delivered in the first fifteen minutes; the rest of the time is spent stitching you up. The incision is usually made horizontally across your lower abdomen, in the pubic hair and out of sight if you later want to wear a bikini. In some situations the cut is made vertically down your belly.

When you awake, assuming you've been knocked out, you'll be surprised that it's over so fast. And at least initially, you'll probably feel more groggy than in pain.

The important thing to remember, however, is that everyone experiences labor differently. Part of the pain comes from our physical build; part of it comes from the level of apprehension we feel. Common emotions following delivery run the gamut from euphoria to sheer relief. Some people feel energized, some feel proud of their accomplishment, some feel tearful, and some feel happy to bask in all the attention. You may feel a burst of love for this new baby you worked so hard to have, but then again you may feel too tired to feel anything else.

Bonding

One word about bonding. It does not necessarily come in a great gush with the birth of the baby. Bonding, feeling intense love for the baby, may not happen suddenly at all. It sometimes occurs outside your awareness. One day you just realize how important this new little baby is.

When my first child was born I expected to feel a great outpouring of love for her. Honestly, though, my first feeling was of relief that I was out of pain. I waited for the tremendous feeling of love to wash over me, and I was embarrassed to admit to the nurse that I didn't feel any different. Isn't a mother *supposed* to feel different? I thought I must be a bad mother because I couldn't identify any feeling for my baby except fondness. It wasn't until days later when she had to be hospitalized for jaundice and was literally out of my hands for twenty-four hours that I suffered tremendous emotional pain. Bonding sometimes occurs instantaneously, but more often than not it comes gradually and without fanfare. If you're being an attentive mother, relax. It'll come; you'll see. Bugles and trumpets don't accompany the happenings of real life.

Advice from Teen Moms

1. "When in labor, try not to be fussy with the nurses; listen to them 'cause they're trying to help you and they wouldn't tell you wrong."
2. "Read about childbirth and ask questions about being a mother and delivery. Go to classes if possible. Be prepared for what will happen when the baby is born and after."
3. "Labor really hurts!"
4. "Labor was hard, painful but exciting!"

5. "Labor was hard on my back."
6. "What was labor like? Well, it was horrible, and all that kept running through my mind was I'm not going to do that again for a long, long time!"
7. "Labor can be scary and frightening, but it helps to know as much as you can what to expect."
8. "About as much as you can say about labor is that we all survived it."

CHAPTER 6

After The Birth

You may stay in the hospital for a few hours, or a few days (typically one to three), or a week if you've had a Cesarean section. After a vaginal delivery you'll spend an hour or so in the recovery room; your boyfriend/spouse and family members can be with you then, but you may prefer simply to rest. The nurses will be cleaning up your baby, weighing him or her, and settling him into the nursery.

Let's look at what will be happening to you—physically and emotionally. Then we'll get back to the baby.

Physical Aftereffects

The bleeding that follows childbirth (called lochia) will continue for ten days or more. It will fade from bright red at delivery to a brownish color and then yellow, much as your period does in a week's time. Your uterus will continue to contract as it shrinks close to its former size. The hormone oxytocin is responsible for the painful contractions, and the doctor can give you pain medication if the discomfort gets intense. Every so often a nurse will come by and press on your abdomen. She's helping the uterus contract more, but it's unpleasant nonetheless. Once the staff is content that you're doing okay on your own, they'll stop. They'll be checking your sanitary pad to monitor the bleeding (you don't want to be passing clots), and they may bind your breasts and put an ice pack on them if you don't plan to breast-feed your baby. This may all sound very undignified to you right now, but you'll probably accept it willingly after what you've been through.

I had my first child at a birth center, and the nurse told me I could go home (with the baby) as soon as I urinated without incident. "You mean I have to go to the bathroom today?" I asked. I'd planned to use the bathroom in a few days, but the idea of sitting on a cold toilet at that particular moment was scarier than skydiving. After all that has happened to that part of your body, it's hard to believe your insides won't fall out when you expose them again.

Well, relax. It doesn't hurt to urinate again, except for a quick burning sensation if you've had an episiotomy. Soaking that part of your anatomy in the bathtub helps the swelling go down and the stinging go away. The hardest part will be relaxing enough to use the toilet freely. Running water in the sink sometimes reminds your body what it's supposed to be doing.

Milk for the baby usually doesn't come in until the third day. In the meantime, if you're nursing your baby he or she will be getting valuable colostrum from your breasts. When the milk does come in, you'll know it. Your breasts will feel heavy and full; they'll start to tingle as the milk "comes down." You'll actually feel relief as the baby starts nursing, because full breasts hurt. If you do decide to breast-feed (more about that in Chapter 7), ask the nurse for help. It's hard to figure out how to hold a wobbly newborn and get the nipple into its mouth at the same time. Don't believe anyone who says it all comes naturally.

If you don't want to breast-feed your baby, be sure to tell your doctor so that he can give you medicine to help dry up your breasts. Your breasts will prepare to feed this baby whether or not you plan on exercising the option. Your milk will still come in. The pills will help dry you up, so to speak, but the nurses will probably bind your breasts tightly to discourage them from engorging. Ice packs will help, because when the milk does come in your breasts will burn and throb. You'll run a fever and feel extremely tender, but the feeling will subside in a day or two. (Don't think you'll escape the burning sensation by breast-feeding instead; you'll encounter it anytime you stop breast-feeding.)

In the weeks after delivery you may find yourself sweating more than usual. Nothing is particularly wrong; it just means that your hormone production has dropped and your body is trying to get back to normal. Menstruation will begin again from eight to twelve weeks after delivery, but don't think that you can't get pregnant because you haven't resumed your periods. You can!

After a C-section you'll encounter a longer period of adjustment. Because you have had major surgery, you'll stay a few days longer in the hospital so they can monitor you. The nurses will get you up within twenty-four hours. When you first push yourself into a sitting position, you'll probably be shocked at how weak you are. You wouldn't think such a small incision could cause so much discomfort! I speak from experience. After my C-section (with my last child), I swore I was going to lie in bed the rest of my life. I was afraid that if I stood up my insides would fall out (and I was thirty-four years old!). I finally put my feet on the floor; the nurse held me on one side, my husband on the other. I put my weight down. Well, my insides didn't spill out, but I felt as if my abdomen were on fire. It took several days of walking before I was more comfortable. And it took several days more before I could walk without holding on to my belly.

You'll still bleed vaginally with a C-section (the lining of the uterus is sloughing off), but the bleeding will be lighter and of shorter duration.

You'll be more tired after having had a C-section and won't be allowed to lift anything remotely heavy (nor will you feel like it). Climbing stairs will discourage you, and standing will tire you quickly.

As you're recovering in the hospital, you'll hurt mostly from gas. Actually, gas is a good sign; it means that your intestines are working again, moving food along as they're supposed to. The nurses will give you pills to make you pass gas because it relieves the pain, but it's a little disconcerting to have no control over that process when you have company in the room.

Possible Problems for the Baby

Now, let's talk about the baby. You can keep yours with you in your hospital room or have him (or her) brought from the nursery when you want. But what if there are complications?

Babies who are born prematurely (before thirty-eight weeks) tend to be hospitalized longer, depending on how premature they are. Obviously, the earlier they are born, the more underdeveloped their lungs and major organs will be. Preemies run the risk of respiratory problems and infections. If their lungs are not fully developed, monitors may be used to check (and assist) their breathing. If your baby is premature you'll see all kinds of equipment surrounding him or her. The doctor may order your baby put in an incubator to regulate his body temperature. All infants wear little caps to protect their heads from heat loss.

A baby may develop jaundice because the immature liver cannot filter out the pigment bilirubin, which is released from the red blood cells. The bilirubin builds up to a dangerous level, turning the baby a yellowish color. The doctor will put such a baby in an incubator under a bright light, which destroys the bilirubin so the body can excrete it.

Premature babies cry more frequently, but more quietly, than full-term babies. They are more easily startled, are smaller, and seem more fragile. You may feel angry and cheated with such a baby. Taking care of a preemie requires so much of you; you may think it's not fair that everyone else you know got a nice fat baby and yours is sickly. You may not feel sure you can take care of it properly. You may feel guilty, blaming the baby's condition on something you did or didn't do while you were pregnant. All of these feelings are normal, but you need to talk about them. Your friends and family may be willing to listen, but you also need to express your concerns and fears to professionals who can help you. Your baby may have to stay longer in the hospital, and it's frightening (and heartbreaking) to leave the hospital that first time without your new baby. Your baby needs your love and attention whether or not you can pick him up and cuddle him. He'll learn your voice and your scent; hang in there. When he's healthy enough to be released, the doctor will tell you what to do and what to expect.

Babies born with fetal alcohol syndrome suffer irreversible symptoms, which means the symptoms never go away. They include growth retardation, brain damage, learning disabilities, and hyperactivity. Can you imagine trying to raise a child like that? It's hard enough for most teenagers to cope with the responsibilities of raising a healthy child. Do yourself—and certainly your baby—a favor in your pregnancy by avoiding those chemicals that lead to an addicted baby. You can't just dump a baby you're dissatisfied with on society.

If you have one of these babies, however, get help from professionals. If you're still drinking too much, or abusing drugs, get help for yourself or you stand to lose your child. Getting help through a substance-abuse program won't make you unfit as a mother (if someone responsible is tending your baby in the meantime), but continuing to abuse drugs and alcohol will.

I mentioned earlier that if you have AIDS your baby will more than likely be born with the disease. In general, babies born with AIDS live for two years. They die from secondary infections. If you find that your baby has AIDS, you're going to grow up fast. Your baby won't necessarily be sick enough at first to warrant placement outside your home. You may feel angry and cheated. You may feel guilty if your behavior prior to the baby's birth contributed to the development of AIDS. But on top of everything else, you're probably going to feel grief at your impending loss.

The health department may not get involved in the baby's care unless they have reason to believe you're not giving proper care. As your baby gets sicker, you may need more specialized care. Your pediatrician will be able to advise you when that time comes.

Advice from Teen Moms

1. "Being a mother isn't just holding the cute little baby all the time. It's a lot of responsibility."

CHAPTER 7

Life with This New

Creature

Funny how this new creature, who was so adorable in the hospital, suddenly turns into a monster when you get her home! She slept around the clock for the nurses, and you never heard her cry once except the moment she was born. Now all of a sudden she won't *stop* crying, whether or not you stick a bottle in her mouth or wrap her in a clean, dry diaper. What's the matter anyway? In this chapter, let's look at problems you may encounter taking care of your new baby.

Colic

Colic is probably the scariest condition your child can develop. Grown men and women quake at the mere mention of the word.

What is colic? Colic is actually excessive crying; it has been described by some as any kind of inconsolable crying. When nothing physical appears to be wrong with the baby (like being hungry or wet, frightened or sick) and she continues to wail without letup, she probably has colic.

One author asserts that "one out of five babies has colic," so don't think of your baby as abnormal. Doctors don't know what causes colic or why it eventually goes away. That's the good news: Babies do outgrow colic in three months or so.

Having a baby that cries more than usual (and even "normal" babies cry three or more hours a day on and off) can drive you crazy faster than anything I know. Our first child had colic. She was fine the first few days, but suddenly at about one week she started crying nonstop. One of us had to hold her constantly and *walk* while doing so. She cried when we even paused to rest. I'd carry her around all day, testing every so often to see if she'd take a nap in her crib (which she wouldn't). As soon as my husband came in from work I'd hand her over, saying, "It's your turn now; I'm going to bed." He'd take over as long as he could stand it.

We did this all day and through the night, though Michal finally fell asleep for half an hour or so sometime during the night. She was quiet only if we walked, rode in the car, or fed her. Imagine my delight when a relative came by to visit, and Michal went right to sleep in her arms. When that continued to happen each time this woman visited, however, I started feeling jealous and then lost faith in my ability to take care of my child. What did this woman know that I didn't? Did my own baby like her better than she liked me?

Well, let me assure you that a colicky baby is not rejecting you. Doctors are discovering that these babies are just hypersensitive for no particular reason. Or at least, for no known reason. Babies don't develop colic because you're a nervous mother or because you're too young. They don't develop it because of food allergies or indigestion (though they do develop gas from prolonged crying). Babies don't develop colic because something traumatic happened to them outside your awareness.

Since we can't explain colic, quit blaming yourself—or the baby—and let's look at some concrete things you can do to help. First of all, when your baby cries, pick her up. You can't spoil a newborn, no matter what your Great-aunt Hilda says. Check whether the baby needs a diaper change or is hungry (and remember that a newborn eats as often as every two hours in the beginning). If nothing seems to be wrong, accept that your baby just cries more than others do. All babies have different temperaments, which predisposes some to cry more than others. Some babies are slow to adapt to change, and some are more negative than others. You won't readily believe this about your first child, but with a second child you'll find that he may be nothing at all like your first. Babies are all different. Some babies "fit" better with you, matching your own temperament, than others. Whatever the case, just accept the baby on its terms. (Believe me, that's easier said than done.)

Remind yourself that colic goes away of itself in three months. Rock the baby. Put her in a baby swing, drive around in your car (with the baby secure in her car seat), or just sit in a rocking chair.

Carry the baby in a Snugli (one of those papoose-like things that tie onto your chest) and continue doing your chores. Sometimes the baby just likes to be near you, listening to your heart.

Appeal to only one of your baby's senses at a time. Don't try everything at once. If it's night, consider the darkness of the room. Either brighten the baby's area or, if the lights seem to bother her, darken it. Try playing lullabies or, if the room is already noisy, turn down the sound. Stroke the baby. Some babies like to be massaged (there are many good baby massage books in the library), but some become overstimulated by it. Try first one thing, and then something else if that fails. But don't do too much at once; it will only make her cry harder.

Believe it or not, some infants like the sound of the vacuum cleaner. When all else failed and I felt ready to drop dead from sleep deprivation, I used to place the vacuum cleaner near the baby's crib and then take a nap. The constant hum put Michal to sleep every time, and as soon as I turned it off, she roused.

If your nerves are wearing thin because your baby is so demanding, get some help. Ask your mother to come over, let your husband take over, or call a visiting nurse (provided to teenagers by many hospitals) to give you a break or some advice. If you feel like striking the baby, call an abuse hotline if no one (neighbor or relative) is available immediately to take over. You can permanently damage a baby by shaking it or hitting it. You can easily kill the baby in one fleeting moment of anger.

Sleep

But maybe you'll take home a contented little person who won't spend the greater part of each day crying. Just remember that all newborns are supposed to sleep between sixteen and seventeen hours the first few days. As the weeks go by your baby will stay awake longer. Newborns awaken every few hours (usually not more than three) to eat, whether you're breast-feeding or bottle-feeding; they can't eat enough at one time to stay full for longer than that. If anyone develops a sleep disturbance at this point, it'll be you, not the baby. You (or someone) has to get up throughout the night to feed him, and if you have trouble getting back to sleep, you'll quickly get cranky. Mothers are a help here, if your husband needs his sleep to work. Some babies start sleeping through the night as early as two months; others take longer. Some sleep through the night from the beginning. It doesn't mean you're a better or worse mother for having a baby that sleeps a lot. Just be prepared to give up a regular sleep pattern yourself, and have some help when needed.

Feeding

If the baby doesn't nurse (whether it's at your breast or on a bottle), call your doctor. An infant (particularly a newborn) can't go very long without eating.

Speaking of feeding your baby, what are the relative advantages of bottle-feeding and breast-feeding? With bottle-feeding the important thing to remember is that you have to sterilize all the equipment—that means the bottles, the nipples, and even the water that's used to mix with the formula. If your baby wakes up and is screaming to be fed, you'll have to endure some hairy moments while you struggle to quiet a hungry infant and do all that sterilizing. The formula has to be warm, of course, and if you use a microwave to heat the bottle you not only diminish the nutritional content, but you can't readily tell how hot the stuff is.

Don't dilute the baby's formula to make it go further. If you don't have enough money to feed the baby, go to Human Services or a family planning clinic and explain your predicament. They'll help you get the money needed to buy milk and formula. Diluting the formula weakens the nutritional value; babies have starved because of this.

An advantage of bottle-feeding, aside from the convenience for others when you're not available, is that you can readily determine just how much your baby is drinking.

The biggest problem with breast-feeding is orchestrating the whole thing. You should cradle the baby in a half-upright position. When the baby is brought close to your breast, he'll root around for the nipple, and when he finds it he'll know just what to do. Make sure he takes the whole nipple in his mouth; he won't express any milk if he only latches onto the tip. It initially hurts when the milk "lets down," but that's followed by a very pleasant sensation (if you allow it to be pleasant) as the baby nurses. There's nothing abnormal about feeling pleasure from a nursing infant. Actually, what is happening is that that old hormone oxytocin is coming into play again. As the baby nurses, your body releases oxytocin, which helps your uterus contract and is responsible for the pleasurable sensation. Oxytocin is also released in orgasm.

Babies don't breathe through the mouth, so be sure your breast doesn't block your baby's nostrils. If it does, press against your breast with a finger to give him breathing room.

The drawback to breast-feeding is that it's more difficult to assess how much the baby has taken in. Your doctor will advise you if the baby seems to be losing weight or languishing, which is an important reason to keep all well-baby appointments. In general, if a baby nurses off your breasts for at least five to ten minutes each he's probably getting adequate nourishment.

If you do decide to breast-feed, I suggest you pick up a book on the subject so you can check out any problems that develop. Breast-feeding does not make for saggy breasts; pregnancy itself contributes to changes in the breasts. Going without a bra also ruins the underlying muscle of the breast. So don't give up on breast-feeding simply because you think you'll lose your shape. That's not so.

Depression

Everyone (who'll admit it) feels some degree of depression after the baby comes. For me, the pregnancy was depressing because I lost so much control over my body; so I didn't experience a great deal of depression after the baby came. Nonetheless, I can't say that I didn't feel down from time to time with all my new responsibilities or because I couldn't come and go as I pleased. Don't be alarmed if you do get depressed.

If you're a single mother you'll have an even tougher job trying to be both mother and father (which is impossible). You'll have twice the responsibilities of other moms and half the assistance. Small wonder if you get depressed. Some teens miss the limelight; Now the baby gets all the attention. Some get depressed simply because they're so tired, or things didn't turn out as they expected. It's not abnormal to be depressed, but it *is* a problem if the depression doesn't lift or if you can no longer function.

Postpartum depression is normal in part because of your altered hormones, and in part because of the letdown of the moment. It's similar to the feeling when the holidays are over, or when the last present under the tree has been opened. All that is normal, and women bounce back if they get some help and some rest.

But another kind of depression becomes chronic and

does not go away. You cannot get out of bed (or you don't want to), and you won't attend to the baby as well. If you find yourself feeling this deep a depression, call your doctor, your school nurse, or a family member to take you to a mental health clinic. They can find you someone to see (if they don't know of a mental health clinic in your area) by looking in the Yellow Pages of the phone book under Marriage and Family Counseling or Mental Health. If you're desperate, call the suicide hotline in your phone book. The number is usually on the inside cover.

Depression is like nausea in early pregnancy: Not all women get it. If you don't *expect* it, you may not *get* it. Don't sit around anticipating depression. You may enjoy motherhood so much (or be so busy) that you don't notice that it's an inconvenience at times.

If you do develop a depression that requires treatment, don't compound your situation by blaming yourself. It's not your fault. Sometimes hormones are to blame for messing up your body chemistry. Appropriate medication may easily rectify the imbalance.

If you find yourself feeling jealous of the baby, don't be too hard on yourself. It happens to us all. Here's this new little creature, keeping you awake all night, demanding all the attention, and getting it! Whereas *you* were the center of attention during your pregnancy, now you have to give up the limelight—never to get it back. (That's another downside to being an adult.) When people came to visit our first child, they brought all kinds of gifts for the baby. While I appreciated the baby things, a not-so-very-nice part of me wanted to shout, "Well, didn't you bring anything for *me*?"

Advice from Teen Moms

1. "Read books and talk to other parents so you'll know what to expect from the different stages of child development."
2. "Don't give up; it gets a lot easier."
3. "Don't blame the child. YOU did this, not the child. You have to take responsibility."
4. "Realize that you can never go back to how your life used to be."

The hardest thing to get used to was . . .

- "the fun was over."
- "how much responsibility I had."
- "waiting on the baby hand and foot; having to guess what was wrong with him because he couldn't tell me."
- "not being able to come and go as I did before."
- "old friends not understanding the meaning of responsibility, so it was almost impossible to do things with them."
- "getting up at all hours during the night."
- "the crying."
- "trying to keep diapers and formula."

CHAPTER 8

And Now What Do I Do?

Learning to stay at home is no doubt one of the least appealing aspects of motherhood. All of a sudden, in one fell swoop, you have this new little creature to take care of and the responsibilities *never go away*! It never ceases to amaze me that I went to the hospital one afternoon and came back the next day with an infant. Almost as if I'd purchased her in the hospital dispensary, only I couldn't take her back if she didn't turn out as expected. One day I was just a woman; the next day I was a mother!

No matter what your earlier teen years were like, those days are over now. If you were carefree, stopping in every so often for family meals, you're not going to be carefree any more. A baby needs its meals on time every day from here on out, and you're responsible for providing them. If you once partied every weekend, you're not going to have the energy to do that any more. Funny how everyone (myself included, when I was your age) thought being pregnant was so grown up and exciting (after all, it proved you'd been doing something *sexual*). But once you have the baby, the excitement fades and you've become a *mother* (something entirely asexual and undesirable.)

What's Expected of You

Whether or not you're still excited about being a mother, let's look at your new responsibilities and the baby's needs. Once again (as in labor and delivery), if you know what to expect, you may feel more comfortable.

I had my first child when I was twenty-nine years old. I thought I was too old to be wondering what I would do with her once I got her home, but I wasn't even sure how to hold her, and she was so fragile looking that I was almost afraid to touch her. When my husband and I got her home, we turned up the thermostat to about 80 degrees, thinking she needed to be warmer. We bundled her in blankets because it was winter, and we sat around sweltering ourselves, watching her sleep. Fortunately, our pediatrician caught on and told us to turn down the thermostat before we all died of heat exhaustion. The baby doesn't need a room temperature warmer than 70 degrees, and it doesn't need to be buried under layers of blankets. That was my first lesson; I made many more mistakes. I'm not saying that you as teenagers don't know anything. I'm saying that we all can use some well-worn advice when we're first-time parents, no matter what our age.

One disillusioning thing you'll discover right away is that the baby doesn't know he's here to meet *your* needs. He thinks you exist to meet *his* needs. A baby doesn't come into this world to give us love; he comes expecting everyone in it to give him love. Babies are very self-centered little creatures. All they know at first is their own wants: food, a dry diaper, a soothing environment, a warm body to hold them. They are not separate enough to realize that they can give anything back, or that you'd even expect it. After all, you are only an extension of them.

Any baby needs love, attention, food, and stimulation. Fortunately, he doesn't always know if we're doing something wrong, and he doesn't penalize us for being new at the job.

The baby also needs proper medical attention. You may have a number of questions to ask a visiting nurse (if your own mother doesn't know the answers) about how to care for a newborn. For instance, the umbilical cord dries up and separates between the seventh and sixteenth days. In the meantime, it just hangs out, getting in the way when you're changing the diaper. You have to wash the cord carefully to avoid infection.

Keep all regular doctor's appointments for the baby. In the beginning you'll probably have as many appointments for a well baby as you would for one that was sick. Babies stay healthy because they're seeing a doctor. He'll want to know that your baby is eating enough, gaining weight, and moving about at the scheduled time. He'll know all the shots the baby needs, and when to give them. If money is a problem you can see a doctor at the county health department, but if you can cover the baby on your (or your parents') insurance policy, choose a private physician. It's good to develop a rapport with your doctor so that if the baby gets sick during the night, you'll have someone to call.

You may feel better having the baby sleep in your room (or you may have no other option), but babies make a lot of noise when they sleep. At first, it's nice to have the baby so near, but very soon you'll notice all the little noises and it'll keep you awake. I started sleeping better once I moved Michal out of our room, though it took me a while to trust that she was breathing okay in the other room. I had to keep sneaking in to listen, and if I wasn't sure she was breathing I disturbed her enough to wake her. Then I had a fussy baby on my hands. (This ritual went on for a year.)

Babies prefer to sleep on their stomach, usually with their nose pushed up against something. As long as there is nothing in the crib (like a pillow) that can suffocate them, they'll sleep fine. Excessive worrying won't keep them any safer, but it will deplete your energy, leading to fatigue and a short temper.

There are things you can do to ensure a safe environment for your baby. First of all, buy some of those inexpensive covers and close up all your electrical outlets. It doesn't matter that your infant can't even turn over yet, let alone crawl around on the floor to get into trouble. Do it right from the start; then you don't have to worry about it when she's old enough or mobile enough to get into things. Never leave a pillow in a baby's crib. Since a baby can suffocate under one, why run the risk?

For the same reason, never leave a baby unattended on a waterbed or on a couch where she can suffocate under the cushions.

Don't let the baby have toys that can come apart or that have dangling strings. A baby can strangle on them in a matter of minutes. Babies explore their world through their mouth, so assume that anything your baby can reach will go in her mouth.

If you have knickknacks that are breakable or have small, swallowable parts, put them out of sight. Like the electrical outlets, you never know when your baby is old enough to get into them. Get into the habit of storing dangerous (or valuable) stuff out of sight.

Smoking around a baby is dangerous for two reasons. One, you run the risk of dropping ashes on the baby. Two, and more important, recent discoveries have shown that secondhand smoke leads to an increase in respiratory infections in children. If you can stop (and I realize that smoking is an addiction), you'll be saving your baby's health as well as your own—and a lot of money. Asking others not to smoke around your child may make you unpopular for a while, but does it matter?

As you've probably guessed, adjusting to a baby requires an awful lot of sacrifices. You lose regular sleep, you can't go out much, you never have enough money, and now you're told to quit smoking. Raising a baby is hard work, and at least in the beginning it goes un-rewarded. (Ever heard an infant say thank you, Mom?)

Help with Your Baby

You're not a bad person if you resent the baby's demands on you. If you're shouldering most of the responsibilities yourself, it's understandable. If you're jealous that your boyfriend/spouse doesn't have as much to do as you (or isn't as tied down), that's normal too. Nonetheless, it's not okay to fly off the handle or neglect the baby simply because you feel like it. At such times you need some help, not just advice. So let's see who's out there to help you.

If you get along with your family (and they're reliable), consider calling them first. Perhaps they'll take the baby for a few hours, allowing you to get out for a while. You aren't a hero for staying twenty-four hours a day with your baby. Smart people take breaks. The advantages of using your sister or mother are your familiarity with them and their availability (usually free.) The disadvantages lie in your wearing out your welcome from calling on them too much, and the opportunity it gives them for over-involvement and taking over.

If you have been abused by someone in the family, don't for a moment think the person has reformed (without treatment) and wouldn't bother your baby. Many abused women have told me that their stepfather (or whoever) began to abuse their child when the opportunity presented itself. People who molest children *do not grow out of it.* Keep your baby safe, as you wish someone had done for you. Remember, babies can't tell you what's wrong. They can only cry, so it's up to you to figure out any trouble (from ear infection to trauma). Better to leave your family out of it if there's any risk of trouble.

Aside from your parents, who else is there? What about the baby's father? If you've married him, he's right there and fully capable of doing "his share." You may feel guilty for "trapping" him with your pregnancy or for his having quit school to support you. But he isn't completely blameless for the pregnancy, having contributed half the genes to this baby. Besides, what's done is done. Talk with him about how you're feeling, but don't demand that he take over. People are more apt to lend a hand when they think it's their idea. If you two can't help each other with the baby care, your marriage is already on a bad footing. Raising a baby is not "woman's work." Two parents are needed for the job. If you're fighting over it, talk to a school counselor or a mental health professional. Clinics exist that don't cost a fortune. Look in the Yellow Pages.

What if you didn't marry your boyfriend, but you're still seeing him? Should he help you out, and how? First of all, decide if he's responsible enough to help with the baby's care and if you want his help. As the baby's father, he is responsible for financial support, but that does not always make him a good candidate for baby-sitter. Several teenage girls told me that the most their boyfriends did was buy diapers and formula for the baby. They wouldn't ask for anything more, mostly because they didn't think the guys would hang around to be baby-sitters. "Better to have a guy bring me diapers than no guy at all," one said.

If you're in a school program (whether traditional high school or an alternative program), consider asking a teacher or counselor for advice. Teachers (and I'm one) usually like the students they work with; that's why they're teaching in the first place. They're flattered to be asked questions because it means you consider them important and knowledgeable. If you need advice, or only a pat on the back, look up your teacher or counselor after class. It's hard to nurture a baby, especially if you haven't been nurtured yourself. That doesn't mean you'll never be able to be a loving mother, though. The mere fact that your own parents couldn't nurture you doesn't mean you can't find a nurturing mentor who'll show you about giving love. A teacher or a counselor or an adult from your church can be that mentor for you.

Many hospitals provide visiting nurses to teens, at least for the first few months. Don't get defensive (as one of my students did, thinking the hospital was checking up on her). Get to know the nurse; she can give you valuable advice and probably knows all the resources in your community. Don't assume that your questions are stupid; it's only stupid when you don't ask them.

If you find yourself at the end of your rope, with no

one to help you, call the abuse hotline listed in your phone book. (If no number is identified as a hotline, call the emergency room of any hospital; they can tell you what to do if they can't help you themselves.) Calling Parents Anonymous or an abuse hotline won't "get you in trouble." Your child's welfare is at stake, and if you call someone to keep yourself from hurting the child (out of anger or frustration), you'll be better off. The counselor can talk you through your anger and suggest ways to cool off or get help.

Take some parenting classes to learn more about baby care in the various stages of development. Your school may offer free classes; if not, check out the YWCA, a family planning clinic, your hospital, or your church. Some classes charge a fee, but you might get it waived because of financial need. Many excellent courses are free. You can't know too much about parenting. After all, raising a healthy child is not instinctive for everyone. I was a great mother once I got done making all the mistakes I made with my first child. If you can't find a class, take out some books from the library and read up on baby care. Not knowing all about parenting doesn't mean you're a bad mother. Bad mothers don't bother to look up stuff they don't know.

Advice from Teen Moms

1. "Learn how to take care of your baby."
2. "Don't blame your child for keeping you away from things you want."
3. "You need to get away from the child once in a while."

CHAPTER 9

When Is There Time for You?

So far, we've looked at problems you might encounter after you've brought the baby home. We've looked at the baby's needs and how you can best provide for them. I've warned you that you might feel both pride and resentment with this new creature. In this chapter let's just consider *you*. It won't take much day-to-day baby care to start you wondering, "When is there time for *me*?"

When you're taking care of a baby, particularly a newborn, you won't have enough time for everyone. The baby gets all the quality time because his demands are so pressing. If you're married (or involved in a steady relationship) the guy gets what's left over, and you have next to nothing for yourself.

To make a marriage work, you can't afford to give your husband leftover fragments of your day. Somehow, you have to set aside specific time for him. Then too, you have to look as if you want to spend time with him. Walking around in your nightgown, reeking of spit-up and dirty diapers, will do little to attract him. I know it's hard to nurture a baby all day long (and half the night) and then get all spruced up for a romantic interlude with your husband/boyfriend. That's why you need to have some baby-sitters lined up. But a marriage is also built on quality time, so plan on investing a little in it. Note the time of day when the baby sleeps consistently and plan to spend that time getting reacquainted with your husband. I say "reacquainted" because you may not have noticed him much since the baby came home.

Husbands (at least the supportive ones) are carrying their load too. If they happen to be students as well, they probably don't have much time on their hands. Holding down a job, going to school, and assuming responsibility for a wife and child is quite an undertaking for someone who has just finished being a kid himself. No doubt he's giving up things (sports, time with the guys) to be with you. You're not to feel guilty for his missing out on these things. The important thing is to realize that you're both contributing to the household.

If you can't spend much time in your husband's world any more (because he's out in it and you're stuck at home with the baby), at least spend time finding out what goes on in his world. Talk to him at night about how he's feeling and what he's doing. Don't use this precious time together to complain about your day. Sure, he ought to know that you have it hard too, but the idea is not to compare hardships; it's to find common ground and the opportunity to enjoy each other again.

Resuming Sex

Speaking of enjoying each other again, you'll probably start thinking of sex sooner or later. Sexual feelings don't

go underground just because you're a mother. And childbirth isn't always so painful (or remembered to be so
painful) that sex is shelved for long. Doctors routinely
suggest that you wait six weeks before engaging in sex (in
order for the episiotomy to heal, and to limit the risk of
infection). Will it hurt when you resume? Not typically.
You'll probably feel apprehensive because you'll expect it
to hurt, and you might be uncomfortable if the episiotomy
site hasn't totally healed. You may worry that you'll be all
stretched inside after having had a baby pass through your
birth canal. The vagina is surprisingly resilient; you won't
be all stretched, and you might be even tighter if the
doctor stitched you up afterward. Your only real concern
has to be avoiding another unplanned pregnancy.

Sex is a good way to reconnect with your husband, but
adjust your expectations the first few times. You don't
have to see stars, but likewise you don't want to engage
in sex halfheartedly, always with your ear to the baby's
room.

Don't spend time worrying whether you're still attractive to your husband, or whether others are more
so. If you take pains with your appearance and take an
interest in your husband (and your love life), he'll more
than likely reciprocate your attention.

Pressing for Marriage

Entertaining boyfriends is a trickier situation. If your
current boyfriend is your baby's father, you may have
mixed feelings about not being married to him. Did *he*
not want to marry you, or did *you* reject him? Are you
waiting for him to "shape up"? One girl I know got pregnant a second time, hoping that if she had a boy this time
her boyfriend would agree to marry her. What she ended

up with was two children under the age of two and a part-time boyfriend (who moved in with another teenager when this girl was disagreeable).

Sometimes it's better for the guy to take the additional time to get to know the baby. Usually, though, if the guy is unwilling to assume a parental role in the beginning, he's unlikely to grow more responsible. Adjust your expectations accordingly, and be prepared to feel some bitterness. No, it doesn't seem fair that he can be a part-time father when you're stuck with being a mother around the clock.

But before you try to orchestrate a hasty marriage, consider some things. Does he show an interest in the baby, or is he simply proud of his accomplishment? Does he resent the attention you show the baby, or is he willing to share you? Does he expect the relationship to continue as before and you to be available to party at all hours? Is he abusive? Statistics show that boyfriends who beat their girlfriends will beat their wives too. And if he beats you, what makes you think he won't hurt the baby? Abusive people don't typically make exceptions.

Your baby's father does need to support his child, and if he's not cooperative you need to contact the Department of Human Services. Don't feel as if you're taking something that doesn't belong to you. Having a baby is a joint proposition and should not ultimately affect only the woman.

Maybe your boyfriend contributes diapers and formula and pays medical bills on occasion. Isn't that enough? I don't know the answer to that one. If all you want is someone to help with some expenses, I guess it's okay. But if you're hoping that he'll change and want to marry you after all, you may be in for a disappointment. Only you can decide if you're better off postponing your future for him to grow up.

Dating Again

If your pregnancy was not the product of a steady relationship and you're not even in touch with the baby's father, at some point you'll start dating again. How does a person date when she's taking care of a baby and can't go anywhere without it?

First of all, you can date and take the baby along (though that doesn't give you any time alone with the guy). Or you can ask your mother or sister to watch the baby so that you can go out. If your family thinks you're taking advantage of them, you might consider asking the guy over for dinner (maybe he can help prepare it or bring it) and conversation once the baby is asleep. Of course, you'll want the guy to like your child, but don't start considering him a marriage prospect the first few dates. The good thing about dating is that you get to be with different people to decide what your "type" is. You won't be able to enjoy yourself with a person if you're constantly sizing him up for fatherhood. Besides, he'll sense what you're doing and be out your door quicker than anything.

You're entitled to date; you're entitled to have some fun without the baby's always being there. But you can't shirk your responsibilities as a mother to pursue your pleasures. Line up a sitter or a reliable friend to stay with the baby.

Since you have a baby, everyone knows you're not a virgin. Does that mean that all guys will expect you to sleep with them? Some might, but that doesn't mean much. You always have the right to say no, and I hope you'd think twice before risking another unplanned pregnancy. Once you've started having sex with someone, it's next to impossible to abstain. You can't go backwards in a relationship. Think before you get yourself in that situation, and be sure to read Chapter 10 about birth control and sexually transmitted diseases. If you're sexually responsible and feel good about yourself, you'll be less apt to turn every encounter into a sexual one.

Think of Yourself

Which brings us to the most important part of this chapter: nurturing *yourself*. You've probably heard the old saying "First love thyself" a million times. But what does it mean right now? Well, in order to feel like nurturing someone else, you have to nurture yourself. If you're giving 98 percent to your baby and 2 percent to your boyfriend or spouse, there's nothing left for you. Soon enough the well will run dry. You won't have the energy or the inclination to take care of anyone else. That's why it's so important to do things for yourself during this time.

Nurture your own growth. If you dropped out of school to have the baby, get back into some program. Most schools have alternative classes for pregnant and parenting teens. Work on your GED so that you can complete your high school requirements. Consider a vocational class or a work/training school program. By learning a trade or a skill, by furthering your education, you enable yourself to support you and the baby. Knowing that you will "get by" no matter what makes for self-confidence. School counselors want you to finish your education, so they will do what it takes to help you get back. Call them. Many places have day-care services right on the premises.

You wouldn't have to find a sitter, and you wouldn't be separated from the baby for the whole six hours or so. You can't live on welfare for the rest of your life. Career training is an incentive to getting off government support and breaking the cycle of poverty. Do you realize how many pregnant teenagers had mothers who were pregnant teens themselves? How are you going to break that pattern if you don't present a different life for your child?

If you have finished school and are simply taking a break to raise the baby, develop some hobbies. Even if you have support for the rest of your life, you'll need to do something with your spare time. The babies will not always need your undivided attention. What will you do when their need for you is less?

Try to get a night out with your friends. You need them to remind you that you're still a person, not just a mother. Believe me, after a few weeks of diapers and bottles you'll jump at the chance to be "free" for a night. Which is not to suggest that you can revert to bad habits from earlier times. If you're breast-feeding, whatever you drink or smoke gets in your milk, and the baby gets it too. You can't completely abdicate responsibility either, which means you can't stay out all night or engage in questionable activities. You're still responsible for another human being.

What You've Lost

Spending time with your friends may remind you of all that you're missing now. There *are* losses connected with raising a child. Most notably, you've lost your freedom to come and go. You cannot make decisions without considering that new little creature who shares your life. You've also lost your own childhood; from here on you

have to act like a grownup, which isn't always fun. Some
people think they'll get to relive their childhood when
they have a baby, but more often than not what happens
is that they realize all the things they've missed. You can't
go back and recreate your own childhood; you have to go
forward and provide your baby's childhood. You'll be sad
that your pregnancy cut short your plans to travel or go
to college with your best friend. You're missing out on
opportunities that others now have. And most of all,
you're missing out on the limelight because the baby now
gets all the attention.

If you accept your feelings of loss and jealousy as the
normal reactions that they are, you can deal with them
and move on. If you feel angry that you've giving up so
much, then stop giving stuff up. You can always make
time for your old friends. If you no longer relate (because
of the baby), make new friends through school, church, or
some parenting program. Find an outlet for your energy
other than immersing yourself in the baby. Find out what
makes you special; what are your talents? Give something
back to your community, particularly if you're receiving
welfare assistance. That way, you need not feel so dependent and undeserving. Volunteer at the children's
library. Brush up on your social skills. Remember, when
this baby starts school you're going to be dealing with
teachers all over again but from a different vantage point.
For her sake (and your self-esteem), be able to express
yourself verbally and on paper.

Sometimes on television I see these cute little babies
parading across the screen. They have a roomful of toys
and two doting parents. They have new bedroom furniture
and enough clothes to change outfits three times a day.
It's then that I wonder if I've shortchanged my own kids
by not giving them all that stuff. Don't be swayed by

TV families. Your life is a lot different from "The Brady Bunch." Don't wallow in what you don't have; consider what you do have. Find the joy in this new little creature and realize that being its mother is very special. Your baby loves you more than anything!

Advice from Teen Moms

1. "Once a day or night, find time to do something for yourself—whether it's painting your nails or relaxing in a bubble bath—just something you enjoy *for yourself*."

CHAPTER ◇ 10

Thinking of Doing

It Again?

Many teenage mothers don't set out to get pregnant again but within a year find themselves in the same boat. Other teens think that what the first child didn't do for their love life, the second one will, and they actually try to get pregnant.

You already know how hard it is to raise one baby, particularly if you're doing it on your own. Imagine the problems you'll encounter when you're raising two. Having another infant doesn't make that first child more mature. No, your first child will resent your doing this to him—giving him a sibling who'll take up all your time. He'll still make his demands on you, and then you'll have two infants making equally insistent demands. Who's going to help you?

If you think having another child will make your life better, think again. Are you trying to shore up your relationship with the first baby's father by giving him a second child? Will a second child make him more responsible? What is he likely to do when the demands on his time (and wallet) increase? Imagine the expense of diapering and feeding two kids at once!

What if your new baby's father is someone other than your first baby's father? Who's going to play "the real Daddy," or will you have visiting privileges for the kids with their respective fathers? Which one will you want to marry? How will your family (and unfortunately the neighbors, not that it's any of their business) accept your children having multiple fathers? Will they think you're promiscuous? Will they be right?

If you try to coordinate two fathers' involvement with the kids, will one child end up getting more attention or support than the other? How will you keep that from happening?

And if you do think that making more babies will strengthen your relationships, what is it about bearing (and subsequently raising) a child that's so attractive? Do you think having children is the only thing you can do? If you're a single mother, you already know that bearing a guy's child is not enough to get him to marry you. A woman I know started having children in her teens and didn't quit until she was well into her thirties. "It's what I do well," she told me. "I make babies." Fortunately for her, she had a husband who could support them all, but who's going to help you care for *your* children?

When I spoke with a group of teenagers about birth control, I was shocked at how little they knew. I was even more shocked that the very girls who took sex education classes (and got As in the course) didn't bother to apply what they had learned to their own relationships. Of all the advice I received from teenage moms, most were warnings to use birth control!

Birth Control

Before you get yourself in the same predicament, let's talk about birth control. After all, one little slip-up is all it takes. *Any unprotected act of intercourse can lead to pregnancy*—whether you're recovering from childbirth or not. Some women get pregnant again before they even resume their periods. All it takes is that they've resumed ovulating, and most people don't know whether or not they've ovulated until after the fact. Breast-feeding is no protection against pregnancy. You may hear the myth that breast-feeding suppresses ovulation. Don't believe it. Did you ever notice how many families have several kids all one year apart? How do you think that happened? You never know how long ovulation is suppressed, so always assume that you're fertile.

Do you know what birth control options are available? If not you can read about them in this chapter, but then I urge you to go to a family planning clinic to find out more. If you're on a tight budget, ask about reduced rates for birth control supplies (whether it's pills or condoms). The clinics are just as interested in reducing teenage pregnancies as you may be.

Abstinence, of course, is 100 percent effective in preventing pregnancy. It will also prevent you from catching a sexually transmitted disease. Abstinence is not the same as "pulling out" before ejaculation. Abstinence is just that: not having sex. Of course, if you're married that's not such a great idea.

The Pill

Short of abstinence, the birth control pill is the next best choice. It is almost 100 percent effective when used

properly. You can't take the pills halfheartedly. You have
to take them every day or night (around the same time),
and if you forget more than two in a row you should use a
backup method of birth control.

Unpleasant side effects may accompany the pill. Some
women experience weight gain, nausea, and vomiting. If
you throw up for more than a day or two while taking
the pill, use another form of birth control along with it.
Obviously, if you're not keeping the pill down you're
doing without any protection against pregnancy.

One of my psychology students did a survey of males'
and females' views of birth control. One of her most
fascinating findings was that guys said they would never
use a method of birth control that had side effects linked
to heart damage and high blood pressure, but they had no
idea she was talking about the pill. Whereas they over-
whelmingly said they'd never use such a "method," they
totally supported their women's using the pill. Funny,
huh? The pill, as good as it is, does have some health
risk for women with kidney problems and high blood
pressure. Its advantage is that it's relatively easy (not
messy) to use. Its disadvantages are two: It does carry
risk, and it has to be prescribed by a doctor (which
increases its cost). Pills cost about $12 a month, depend-
ing on the brand you use and whether the clinic gives you
a reduced rate.

The pill offers no protection against sexually transmitted diseases such as gonorrhea or chlamydia, or AIDS.
If you mean to use the pill to uncomplicate your sex life,
realize the dangers that come along with a freer sex life.
You must be doubly certain of your partner's health and
history. The chemicals in the pill can keep you from
creating a baby out of your encounters, but it cannot
destroy any virus that might be transmitted to you.

The IUD

An IUD is another very effective choice in preventing pregnancy. You have to see a doctor to be fitted with an IUD, so you have that initial expense, but it can remain in place in your uterus (where it acts to prevent a fertilized egg from implanting) for a year or two. Some people say that it is painful to have the IUD inserted and that they have heavier than normal bleeding, and more cramping in their periods. The advantage is that you're well protected without having to spend more money each month for protection.

Like the pill, the IUD offers no protection against sexually transmitted diseases, or AIDS.

The Diaphragm

Some women prefer to use the diaphragm, which is a circular rubber cap inserted into the vagina to block sperm from entering the cervix (the entrance to the uterus). You have to be fitted for a diaphragm by a doctor, and then you have to buy it at a pharmacy. If you rely on this method you have to use it *every* time you have sex, no matter whether you think the time is "safe" or not. You must insert the diaphragm before engaging in sexual foreplay because sperm can "leak" into your vagina even before your partner ejaculates. You must leave the diaphragm in place for eight hours after sex. If you take it out immediately, enough sperm are left in your vagina to make it into your uterus.

Use a spermicide with the diaphragm to increase its effectiveness. Check the product for its list of ingredients. Nonoxynol-9 is the most effective spermicide now on the market. It is also effective in lessening (though not eliminating totally) the risk of STDs. Although nonoxynol-9 is the best stuff you can buy, some women find it abrasive, causing itchiness and rashes. If you think you're allergic to this ingredient, talk to your doctor about what other spermicide you can use in its place.

Take good care of your diaphragm. Check it periodically for tears. We have a six-year-old son now because I didn't do that. Don't use petroleum jelly as a lubricant with your diaphragm; the petroleum will damage the rubber. If you need additional lubrication, use K-Y jelly.

There's a knack to getting the diaphragm in place. Make sure you know how to insert it before you leave your doctor's office. A friend of mine wasn't sure how to insert it or how it was supposed to feel inside her when it fitted properly. Consequently, she put it in the way she thought it should go. Nine months later she had her first child. The nurse will be more than willing to show you how to insert the diaphragm. Don't leave the office until you're sure you can copy the procedure.

Does the diaphragm interfere with sex? Can the guy feel it? If the guy knows you have one in place, he'll probably come to recognize its feel. But it won't be an unpleasant sensation if you have it in right.

Another disadvantage of the diaphragm is that you have to be comfortable with your body to use it. If you're squeamish about using tampons, you'll probably not like the diaphragm. And if you don't like it, you probably won't use it. You can't prevent pregnancy by wishes alone.

My sources tell me that the sponge is not effective in preventing pregnancy in someone who has already had a child. Don't even waste your time on this device.

The Condom

The only other reliable method of birth control is the condom, which is also the only method capable of protecting against STDs and AIDS. Notice I didn't say that it *prevents* them. At the moment, it is only safe to say that it's capable of doing so. Condoms break, and slip off. They are not a 100 percent effective means of birth control.

Condoms come in all sizes and textures. If you decide to use the condom, get in the habit of requiring your partner to put it on before there is *any* penile insertion. Make the act of donning a condom a part of your lovemaking. Remember, petroleum jelly causes deterioration in rubber, so don't endanger your condoms by using Vaseline with them.

Your partner must withdraw his penis as soon as he ejaculates. Leaving it inside you may permit the condom to slip off. To prevent pregnancy (as well as STDs) you don't want *any* seminal fluid coming in contact with your vagina.

Condoms are relatively cheap, and they can be purchased in any drugstore, grocery store, or gas-station rest room. If you're more concerned with birth control than your boyfriend is, *you* buy the condoms. But don't carry them around in your purse, or rely on one that your boyfriend has had in his back pocket all week. Heat weakens condoms, causing them to break at strategic moments.

Ideally, men should be responsible enough to provide birth control, but the reality is that you, the woman, get pregnant. Therefore, you should always take precautions whether or not you think your partner should share the responsibility. If you're embarrassed to go to the store and buy a package of condoms, consider how you'll feel when you're back there buying a pregnancy test.

Other birth control methods (and I won't even bother to name them) are not reliable enough to be considered. If you find fault with all the methods I've mentioned so far, you're stuck with abstinence—the most reliable method of all.

I talked about sexually transmitted diseases in Chapter 3 in discussing the complications of pregnancy. I'm referring to herpes, gonorrhea, and chlamydia. Usually women don't show many symptoms of these diseases (except with an active case of herpes), so they don't have them treated. Untreated STDs can forever end your chance of getting pregnant again. They can render you sterile and make you very ill. If you're already pregnant, they can damage your baby at delivery. Don't play around with STDs; they are serious, and they're on the rise because teenagers haven't taken them seriously enough.

The STDs mentioned are bad, but they're treatable (and most are curable). The STD called AIDS, on the other hand, is not curable. *You die from AIDS.* People say, "Well, we're all going to die sometime." Which is true, of course. But the way you die from AIDS complications is something no one would wish on anyone. You don't just die quietly; you deteriorate right before your eyes. You lose control of body functions, and you lose touch with people, who are afraid you'll give them the disease. With AIDS the immune system is destroyed, and the body is no longer able to fight off infections. You ultimately die from Kaposi's sarcoma (a skin cancer), or pneumonia, or some other infection. It is a painful death.

Teenagers notoriously think they're going to live forever, that nothing bad could happen to them. I know because I was a teenager myself, and I believed that. That's why teenagers are most susceptible to AIDS right now. They don't believe it can affect them, so they don't take steps to protect themselves. The HIV virus is passed in bodily secretions, including vaginal fluids. It can be passed in one *single* contact, and once you have the virus there's no going back. There are drugs that can prolong your life, but nothing that can halt the ravages of the disease.

Because the virus is passed in semen, women contract AIDS more easily than men. You can't tell by looking at a person whether he's carrying the HIV virus. Until he starts showing signs of the infections that wreak havoc on his body when his immune system breaks down, he looks like anyone else. It is not true that only homosexuals and drug abusers get AIDS. Heterosexuals and teenagers get AIDS too. The only way to protect yourself is to use a condom and hope that it holds up.

Should you require your partner to have an AIDS test before you have sex? That's up to you; it's your life that can be cut short. If you don't know your potential partner well enough to ask him his sexual history, you don't know him well enough to be having sex in the first place. Remember that you're not just having sex with this guy; you're having sex with everyone he's ever had sex with. If they gave him AIDS, they'll be giving it to you too.

Maybe safe sex is not having sex at all . . .

Advice from Teen Moms

1. "Be careful when having sex."
2. "Use birth control if you choose to have sex."
3. "Use a condom."
4. "Just because you haven't gotten pregnant doesn't mean you don't have to use birth control."
5. "If you wish to have sex, use birth control."
6. "Don't get pregnant again during your teen years."
7. "Don't get pregnant again until you are old enough to have a good job and are mature enough to handle the responsibilities."

CHAPTER 11

Where Did the Time Go?

Even though it feels at first as if you'll be tied down for the rest of your life, soon enough your baby grows up. As he or she grows, he'll begin to need you less. "Good enough" mothers learn to cherish the moments when the baby needs them completely because they're over so quickly. As the baby needs you less, you learn to let go of him too.

Let's talk a little then about your child's changing needs. Children all face the same developmental tasks, but they do not develop at the same rate. Most first-time mothers worry that their child is not developing on schedule and fear that something must be wrong. Probably nothing is wrong; the child is just developing at his own, slower pace. You can't will your child to reach all the developmental milestones on *your* timetable. So it's not always useful to compare notes with your friends about your children's progress.

Following are some stages that children go through,

but don't be concerned if your child is a month or two (or even more) behind in reaching these stages. *All* children start out seeing themselves as the center of the universe. You—the mother—are merely an extension of themselves, which is why all babies are certain you can meet their every need—you and they are one. Babies explore their world through their senses, primarily their mouth. At first everything, no matter how gross it appears, goes into their mouth. They suck on the thing; they chew on it; and often, to our disgust, they swallow it. You might try exploring your house from their perspective sometime. Crawl around on your hands and knees, and check out what's in their line of vision (and within reach).

Getting Around

In the beginning babies are aware of their primary caregiver, usually their mother. They know not only your face but your scent, and they prefer it to all others. They prefer looking at faces and bright colors or bold black-and-white designs. Remember that when you buy baby toys. Babies usually learn first to roll over from stomach to back. The first time it happens is usually an accident, but the child readily seeks to repeat the experience if it doesn't totally startle him and others. Then the baby learns a harder task: to roll from his back onto his stomach. (Some kids do the two in reverse, so don't hold your breath waiting for the right sequence.) Babies sit up at about six months. They crawl around on their bellies before making it up onto their knees. Then, before they can actually propel themselves forward on their knees, they get stuck moving their torso back and forth while their knees remain firmly on the floor. They rock back and forth until one day they suddenly take off. Crawling is a complicated process, believe it or not. Children may pull themselves up into a standing, hanging-on position around eight months. Next they walk around holding onto things (even unstable things, so be alert). Finally, they walk on their own at anywhere from nine to fourteen months. The earlier he walks does not necessarily mean he is smarter. All it may mean is that he has better motor development. Usually, if a child excels in one thing, he's a little slower in another.

My first child sat up on schedule and pulled herself up on schedule, so we were sure she would walk any day after that. But after skipping crawling to try standing up, Michal went back to crawling and didn't take her first steps alone until well after her first birthday. By then I was convinced she was never going to walk. I ignored all the women at work whose kids were early walkers.

Communicating

As to when children talk, that's highly variable too. Our oldest started talking almost as soon as she got teeth. In fact, when I look back on it I'm not sure she wasn't born talking. It seems as if Michal was always talking back to us. Our next child hardly said a word until her second birthday, and then she began talking in sentences. No baby talk for her. In fact, much to my dismay, her first complete sentence was, "I'm mad at you, Mommy."

Some children go through a stuttering phase; others don't. Two children I know talked babyishly at their third birthday parties. I was convinced they were both delayed in speech development. Six months later Alex is talking up a storm, speaking clearly and distinctly and with a great vocabulary. Nicholas is still using baby talk and is even hard for my six-year-old to comprehend. Which one is normal? Perhaps both are. It just goes to show how difficult it is to predict how kids will turn out.

Developmental Problems

Doctors seem to believe that all mothers are hysterics who live to worry about their offspring. Actually, I know from experience that it's easy to get caught up in worries that your child is not normal. Usually, I tell mothers to calm down and quit scrutinizing everything their child does or doesn't do. However, mothers should be advocates for their children and should be willing to consider when things are not quite right with them. Sometimes the doctor, who sees the child for a few minutes at most in the examination room, fails to notice a developmental problem. If you see behavior you think is strange and the doctor doesn't mention it, bring it to his attention. If he thinks it's nothing, no harm done. If it is significant, you've saved a lot of time for both the doctor and your child.

As a rule, though, kids develop according to their own inner timetable, which means when they're good and ready. Babies cut teeth as early as three months or as late as one year and older. Usually, the early teethers are the first ones to lose their baby teeth (by the age of five). Cutting teeth early means nothing unless you're breast-feeding and getting bitten regularly.

Beginning to Think

After the infant stage of experiencing their world through their mouth, children go through a concrete stage of thinking in which everything is taken literally. If you say to a three-year-old, "Oh, I'm just not myself today," she might respond quite seriously, "Then who are you?" If you pour the same amount of juice into glasses for two kids, but one glass is tall and skinny and the other short and fat, the kid with the tall glass will think he's gotten more juice. Realizing that kids think this way may help you deal with their (to you) odd behavior at times.

At about seven (and remember, this isn't a hard and fast rule), kids develop more abstract thinking and can understand much more. The timing of this stage is why your child may not be ready to read before seven or can add and subtract only by using counters or coins.

If you want to stay on top of your child's stages of development, I suggest you pick up a good baby-care book. Anything by Dr. Benjamin Spock (who is not the Mr. Spock of the "Star Trek" shows) is good. An excellent book to help you survive early parenting is Vicki Lansky's *Practical Parenting Tips*. Don't drive yourself and your child crazy by comparing notes with every mother who has a child your child's age. Children *do not* develop the same. Have an idea about what takes place when, but don't expect your child to comply.

Enjoy these years with your baby. Keep a journal of cute comments your toddler makes or funny things he or she does. Once the baby is off and running, you can look back over those earlier times and remember. Take a lot of pictures, and have someone take pictures of you and the baby together. You'll probably want to remember how you looked back then. If you don't have a camera (or a good enough one), keep it in mind for a shower gift or a Christmas gift. Just as you can't spoil a newborn, you can never take too many pictures. Your baby will change dramatically from month to month, and without pictures it's easy to forget the little (peaceful) creature she once was.

A Mother's Feelings

How will you feel about your child as she grows? Sometimes it depends on your circumstances. If you're having trouble providing for yourselves or your baby is always sick, you may feel more negative emotions than positive. All mothers experience both kinds of feelings. Sometimes you'll be amazed how bright your child is—possibly the smartest creature alive. Then you may be angry that this smart creature does such stupid things, like using your best lipstick to draw mouths on her stuffed animals. You'll no doubt feel alternately overprotective and too indulgent. You'll wish your child were older (and hence less of a burden), and you'll wish he were a baby again so you could stash him in his crib to sleep.

You'll have a lot of different feelings for this child, and you'll continue to feel all these conflicting emotions until the day you die. You never stop being a mother! The one thing you'll have in common with other "good enough" mothers (a term I borrowed from the child psychologist Bruno Bettelheim, who holds that no mother is totally "good," just "good enough") is that you'll think about your child constantly. For many years your life will be tightly bound up with your child's, even if it's not with the child's father.

Day Care

If you move back into the workforce, what will you do with your child? Welfare will more than likely foot your day-care bill if you use a licensed facility and if you're either going back to school or working in a reputable business. Check with your county health department or family planning clinic for specific details.

You may wonder how you're supposed to find a "good" day-care center for your child. First of all, you'll want (and need, if Welfare is picking up the tab) a licensed facility. Your social worker should have a list of licensed homes. Visit the centers (not always at the staff's convenience) to check the environment. What is the ratio of children to staff? If it's greater than eight to one (or twelve to one in an older age group), your child will not get much individual attention. Problems may go unnoticed. What is the atmosphere? Do the teachers and administrators welcome your interest, or do they try to steer you away from certain areas or allow you to visit only at set times? How do they treat you? As a kid yourself? Or do they listen to you and take your concerns seriously? How do they relate to your child? Do they try to push her into activities, or are they flexible, letting her come to them? Do they seem knowledgeable, or do they act as if they know *everything*?

Make a list of questions you want to ask so that nothing goes unanswered. Try not to be intimidated by those in positions of authority. Remember, you're hiring them to care for your child. You want to feel good about your decision.

Is the center in a good location? Is it on a busy street? Is it clean? What are the toys like? Think of what's important for your child, and then check out a variety of day-care centers from which to choose.

Once you have found a center that you and your child both like, always accompany your child (no matter how old he or she gets to be) to the classroom. Some places have a drive-through front entrance, and you're told to stay in the car while the staff walks your child in. Nonetheless, you need to know what's going on in the center, and you want to convey to your child that he's worth your taking the time to go with him. Your child will probably feel anxious about your leaving at first, particularly if he's older than eight months (which is the age when most kids experience "stranger anxiety" and worry about having you out of sight).

If may break your heart to leave your child crying, but try to remember that he needs some independence and you're leaving him in capable hands. Learn to recognize signs of abuse (sexual as well as physical). If you find any strange bruises on your child when you pick him up, call them to the teacher's attention. Evaluate the explanation. If your child suddenly starts talking too precociously about sex (seeming to know things that he shouldn't know), be concerned. If he's terrified of the center (after having liked it), be concerned. If he starts having nightmares or fearing to go to bed, be concerned. Children regress, revert to more babyish behavior, when they are stressed. It may be only because you have another child or a new boyfriend or your routine is disrupted. But it may be because your child is being abused. If you see an increase in aggressive behavior, try to find the reason. In all the above examples it is reasonable to suspect abuse, but there can be more than one explanation.

Will your child become more attached to his day-care worker than to you? Children do become attached to their caregivers, and that's well and good in most cases. You want them to like the people they spend a great part of their waking hours with. *You, however, will never be replaced!* Your child may adore his teacher, but you are still his mother, and as long as you treat him well (and sometimes even if you don't), he'll shower you with devotion too.

Getting Along with Parents

Now that you feel more like an adult and your child is growing up, how's your relationship with your folks? Being a teenage mother usually necessitates renegotiating that relationship. I know it sounds trite, but I'll say it anyway: If you want to be treated as an adult you have to act like one. That means not taking advantage of your parents when you need money or a baby-sitter. If you count on them to meet all your needs, you're still a kid yourself. Adults still need their parents, but they can rely on themselves too.

Are your parents good grandparents? Do they treat your child fairly? Do they discriminate between their grandchildren if they have more than one? How do you handle that? Do you expect your child to be the favorite? How do you handle advice they may give you about raising the baby? Do you automatically turn a deaf ear, or do you take everything they say as gospel? (Both approaches have problems.) Adults listen more than they speak (or they ought to, anyway). Your parents, you've probably discovered, are neither the gods nor the monsters you once thought they were. Weigh what they say, and be glad if they're involved with you. Be proud of yourself, though, and stand firm in your beliefs. If that means telling your mom or dad, "Let me handle it," be sure you're capable of doing so.

Believe that most people want to be as good parents as they can be. You're a mother, and you want to be the best you can, don't you? Isn't that why you've read this book?

A positive, upbeat attitude goes a long way to foster the kind of environment that brings good things. Hang in there. It's hard work being a "good enough" mother; you deserve a pat on the back. Also honor your parents if they did even a half-decent job of raising you. You'll see them differently when you're an adult. Chances are, you may act like them too. I was never so astonished as I was the first time I said to my kids, "Just wait till you grow up and have kids of your own!" My mother used to say that twenty years earlier, and I swore I would never make such an asinine remark to *my* kids. But history repeats itself, which is scary if you come from an abusive family. Take care that you always treasure your children. They're counting on you.

Advice from Teen Moms

1. "Let your baby grow up. Don't try to keep it a baby forever."
2. "Keep a scrapbook, a journal, a photo album full of pictures—or all three—to remember this time."
3. "You never repeat that first time. Even if you do it again."

CHAPTER 12

How Do I Know I'm Doing Okay?

How will you know if you're doing a good enough job raising your child? Give yourself a quick test; read over the following questions and decide for yourself. Then read the suggestions on baby basics to have on hand, whom to call with problems, and ways to discipline your child.

AM I ABLE TO MEET MY BABY'S NEEDS?

1. Can I afford infant formula without diluting it to stretch it out?
2. Do I keep all doctor appointments, no matter how costly or inconvenient?
3. Do I show my baby love through my time and attention?
4. Have I sought to make his or her living environment as safe as possible?

5. Do I know CPR techniques and the Heimlich maneuver for children?
6. Do I know how to take my baby's temperature (rectally and under the arm)?
7. Do I refrain from smoking in my home and ask others not to smoke around the baby?
8. Have I borrowed or bought all necessary baby equipment? (See list of baby basics at the end of the chapter.)
9. Do I have someone to turn to when I need help with the baby?
10. Am I free to call him or her at any hour of the day or night?
11. Can I control my temper when the baby "acts up"?
12. Is there a pattern of abuse in my family, and can I speak up in my baby's behalf, if necessary?

AM I ABLE TO MEET MY OWN NEEDS?

1. Do I have a life apart from motherhood?
2. Do I have hobbies that I still work on?
3. Do I see friends without the baby?
4. Have I set some positive short-term goals?
5. Have I finished school or am I working toward my diploma?
6. Can I name things for which my baby would be proud of me?
7. Can I support myself and the baby?
8. Do I know how to seek financial assistance?
9. Do I take an interest in my appearance?
10. Do I stay informed of current events and community news?

11. Can I do all these things and provide for the baby at the same time?

CAN I FIND FULFILLMENT IN A RELATIONSHIP?

1. Have I reconciled the relationship with my baby's father?
2. Is he supporting me?
3. Do I have time to give to a relationship *and* the baby?
4. Do I know what birth control options I have?
5. Do I take precautions against AIDS and STDs?
6. Do I believe those diseases wouldn't affect *me*?
7. Do I need a boyfriend or husband only for financial support?
8. Do I need a boyfriend or husband in order to feel complete?
9. Do I enjoy being with a guy even if I'm not going out on an expensive date?
10. Do I treat myself with respect and expect others to do so?
11. Am I proud of my accomplishments?

If you can answer yes to the last two questions, you've already learned a lot. You *should* be proud, because teenage motherhood is no small undertaking.

THINGS TO HAVE ON HAND FOR THE BABY

diapers (3 dozen cloth and diaper pail, or 2 boxes Newborn disposable diapers)

T-shirts (6 to 12)

drawstring nightgowns (6 to 12)

sleepers (3 to 6)

sweaters
lightweight jacket ⎫ depending on the season
snowsuit coverall ⎭

receiving blankets (1 dozen)

baby blankets (3)

crib sheets (3 to 5) You only need the fitted bottom sheet.

bumper pad (to tie around edges of crib)

mattress

mattress pad

formula

baby bottles with infant-size nipples (1 dozen)

toothpicks to unclog bottle nipples

rectal thermometer

nasal suction bulb (may come in hospital newborn package)

K-Y jelly

baby lotion

baby powder

baby bath liquid

cornstarch (straight from the grocery shelf; it's great for diaper rash)

Vaseline

diaper rash ointment or Butt's Paste

infant Tylenol drops (*never* give an infant or child aspirin; it could lead to Reyes Syndrome, a life-threatening condition)

car seat

stroller

crib

humidifier

playpen

high chair

books on child care and breast-feeding

Optional

portable crib

Snugli baby carrier

mobile

rattles

baby swing

walker

rocking chair (for you as well as a baby-sized one)

small tub for baths

bathtub ring for a baby who can sit up by himself (but *never* leave a baby unattended in water) baby towels with hoods

tapes of recorded sounds or lullabies (our daughter quieted to the sounds of whales singing)

nightlight

assorted baby books (good ones include *Mother Goose*, Margaret Wise Brown's *Goodnight Moon* and *Runaway Bunny*, the Beatrix Potter *Peter Rabbit* books, *Pat the Bunny*)

WHAT TO DO ABOUT PROBLEMS

Call Your *Mother* When . . .

- you need a baby-sitter.
- you don't know how to give your baby a bath, pin a diaper, etc.
- you're not sure how to dress your baby for the day.
- you need another hand.
- you've run out of diapers or formula.
- you want to come visit for dinner.
- you want someone to talk to.
- your baby first turns over on her own, smiles her first smile, etc.

Call Your *Doctor* When . . .

- your baby runs a fever (above 100°) for more than an hour.
- your baby coughs and gasps for breath (after you've determined nothing is obstructing the airway).
- your infant isn't eating.
- your infant is vomiting continuously or having nonstop diarrhea.

- your child's behavior seems unusual (too listless or agitated).
- your baby cries for more than an hour straight and cannot be comforted.
- your newborn has a yellow color.
- your baby has a seizure.
- you suspect physical or sexual abuse (have found bruises or injuries on the baby), or have intentionally hurt your baby yourself. Worry about your guilt and possible punishment later. Get the baby to the doctor or hospital *now*.

SUGGESTED METHODS OF DISCIPLINE

- *Be the perfect role model.* Children learn first by observing the people close to them. What is *your* behavior saying to them?
- *Encourage good behavior by rewarding the good and ignoring the bad* (as long as the bad isn't dangerous). Use positive reinforcement (praise and rewards) and negative reinforcement (removal of privileges).
- *Associate your child's name with praise, not reprimands.*
- *Use physical punishment sparingly, if at all, and only in extreme circumstances* (e.g., to discourage the child from running back into the street). When you strike a child, you are saying it is sometimes okay to hit. Hitting tends to breed more aggressive behavior; it also destroys the child's trust in you.

For Further Reading

Charlish, Anne, and Holt, Linda Hughey. *Birth-Tech*. New York: Facts on File, 1991.

Hales, Dianne, and Johnson, Timothy. *Intensive Caring*. New York: Crown Publishers, 1990.

Hyde, Margaret O., and Forsyth, Elizabeth H. *AIDs: What Does It Mean to You?* New York: Walker & Co., 1989.

Jones, Carl. *After the Baby Is Born*. New York: Dodd, Mead & Co., 1986.

Kitzinger, Sheila. *The Complete Book of Pregnancy and Childbirth*. New York: Alfred A. Knopf, 1989.

Levert, Suzanne. *AIDs: In Search of a Killer*. New York: Julian Messner, 1987.

Pelusco, Emanuel and Lucy Silvay. *Women and Drugs*. Minnesota: Compcare Pub., 1988.

Poliakin, Raymond. *What You Didn't Think to Ask Your Obstetrician*. Chicago: Contemporary Books, Inc., 1987.

Redshaw, Rivers, and Rosenblatt. *Born Too Early*. London: Oxford University Press, 1985.

Russell, Keith, and Niebyl, Jennifer. *Eastman's Expectant Motherhood*. Boston: Little, Brown & Co., 1989.

Tapley, Donald, and Todd, W. Duane, eds. *The Columbia University College of Physicians and Surgeons Complete Guide to Pregnancy*. New York: Crown Publishers, 1988.

Weissbluth, Marc. *Crybabies: Coping with Colic*. New York: Arbor House, 1984.

Williams, Phyllis. *Nourishing Your Unborn Child*. New York: Avon Books, 1982.

Index